● **soho** theatre

Dialogue Productions and Mercury Theatre Colchester in association with
Soho Theatre present

Wedding Day at the Cro-Magnons'

by Wajdi Mouawad

translated by Shelley Tepperman

First performed at Mercury Theatre Colchester on 26 March 2008

Soho Theatre is supported by

  Bloomberg

Performances in the Lorenz Auditorium
Registered Charity No: 267234

Dialogue Productions and Mercury Theatre Colchester in association with Soho Theatre present

Wedding Day at the Cro-Magnons'

by **Wajdi Mouawad**
translated by **Shelley Tepperman**

Neyif	**Patrick Driver**
Souhayla	**Karina Fernandez**
Neel	**Mark Field**
Gentleman	**Jeremy Killick**
Nazha	**Beverley Klein**
Nelly	**Celia Meiras**

Director	**Patricia Benecke**
Designer	**Sara Perks**
Lighting Designer	**Hansjörg Schmidt**
Music & Sound	**Nikola Kodjabashia**
Assistant Director	**Susannah Pack**
Production Manager	**Matt Noddings**
Company Stage Manager	**Sarah Gentle**
Assistant Stage Manager	**Rebecca Raggett**
Design Assistant (Costume)	**Lucy Wilkinson**
Education Consultant	**Laura McFall**
Casting	**Nadine Hoare**

Technical Manager	**Nick Blount**
Head of Lighting	**Christoph Wagner**

Dialogue Productions would sincerely like to thank:

Wajdi Mouawad, Michel Simard, Shelley Tepperman, Baron and Baroness Benjamin de Rothschild, Firoz Ladak, Anne-Aimée Frances, Colin Hicks, Marie Morin, Lisa Goldman, Mark Godfrey, Nina Steiger, Dee Evans, Susannah Pack, Sirine Saba, David Gallagher, John Kenton, Matthew Scott, Simona Hughes, Robert Merry, Tina Temple-Morris, Eva Koch-Schulte, Janet Gordon, David Harradine, Kazan Restaurant, Victoria and everyone at Soho Theatre and the Mercury Theatre Colchester.

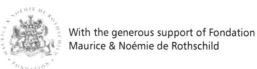

With the generous support of Fondation Maurice & Noémie de Rothschild

LOTTERY FUNDED

Cast

Patrick Driver Neyif

Theatre includes *Othello* (Salisbury Playhouse), *Reverence – A Tale of Abelard & Heloise* (Southwark Playhouse), *Ma Rainey's Black Bottom, London Assurance, Volpone* (Royal Exchange Manchester), *No, It Was You* (Arcola Theatre), *Highs and Lows* (Hackney Empire), *Hunger, Imperfect Librarian, Theatre Dream, Half Machine*, the award-winning *Icarus Falling* and *Poseidon* (Primitive Science), *Christie in Love* (Edinburgh Festival).

As Joint- Artistic Director of Dialogue Productions, he has co-produced, co-translated and appeared in *The MC of a Striptease Act Doesn't Give Up* (Edinburgh & Kilkenny Festivals, UK, US & European tours), *Top Dogs* (Southwark Playhouse & UK tour), *Heroes Like Us* (Edinburgh Festival), *Merlin* (Riverside Studios), *Helter Skelter* (Bush Theatre) and was assistant director on their production of *Monsieur Ibrahim and The Flowers of the Qur'an* (Bush Theatre, Edinburgh and tour).

Television includes *The Whistleblowers, Holby City, The Office, The Last Chancers, Worst Week of My Life, Peepshow, Grass, The Bill, Doctors, People Like Us, My Hero, Ghosts* and *Mr Charity*.

Karina Fernandez Souhayla

Theatre includes *Macbeth* (Bristol Old Vic), *Mrs Pat* (Theatre Royal, York), *Woody Allen's Murder Mysteries* (Croydon Warehouse), *Crocodile Seeking Refuge* (Lyric Hammersmith), *Bites* (The Bush Theatre), *Shopping and F***king, Blue Heart* (Royal Court), *Trips* (Birmingham Rep), *Cool Water Murder* (Belgrade Theatre), *The Boy Who Left Home* (Lyric Hammersmith and national tour), *Romeo and Juliet* (Pleasance Theatre and national tour), *Passion* (Chelsea Theatre), *Dealing with Clair* (Union Theatre), and *Hamlet* (Gatehouse Theatre).

Television and film includes *Happy Birthday Shakespeare, The Forsyte Saga, The Return, Gabriel* and *Happy Go Lucky*.

Mark Field Neel

Theatre includes *Mad Funny Just* (Theatre 503), *Vincent River* (Trafalgar Studios), *The Promise* (Mercury Theatre Colchester), *Carrie's War* (Sadler's Wells), *24 Hour Plays* (The Old Vic), *When Five Years Pass* (Arcola), *An Inspector Calls* (RNT International Tour, Dir: Stephen Daldry), and *A Night Of Conscience* (St James, Piccadilly).

Film includes *Brideshead Revisited (2008)*.

Radio includes *Under Milk Wood, Herons*, and *The Tempest*.

In 2005 Mark was awarded the Alan Bates bursary award for outstanding newcomer.

Jeremy Killick Gentleman

Theatre includes *Parts for Machines that do Things* (Sheffield Theatres and Third Angel), *Where from Here?* (Third Angel), *The World in Pictures, Bloody Mess, The Travels, First Night* (Forced Entertainment), *Poseidon* (Primitive Science), *Copenhagen* (Michael Codron), *The Tempest* (ESC Education), *Pygmalion* (American Drama Group), *Twentieth Century* (New End Theatre), *Iron Dreams* (Pop-up), *A Kiss in the Gutter* (Traverse Theatre), *Cartagena* (Royal Theatre, Northampton), *A Kind of Immigrant* (Graeae), *Broken Heads* (Battersea Arts Centre), *Twelfth Night* (Forest Forge), and *Why Is Here There Everywhere Now?* (Lumiere & Son).

Television and film includes *POW, Cardiac Arrest, Crime Limited* and *My Wrongs #345-647*.

Beverley Klein Nazha

Theatre includes *Restoration* (Headlong Theatre Company), *The Holy Terror* (Duke of York's Theatre), *Camille* (Lyric Hammersmith), *Six Characters Looking for an Author* (Young Vic Theatre), *Romeo and Juliet, The Villain's Opera, Summerfolk* (National Theatre), *Sarrasine* (Lyric Hammersmith), *The Threepenny Opera* (Donmar Warehouse), *A Judgement in Stone* (Gloria), *Piaf* (Oldham Coliseum), *Nasty Neighbours, The Woman Who Cooked Her Husband* (Snarling Beasties), *Torch Song Trilogy* (Manchester Library Theatre), *Stevie* (Guildford Theatre), and *Educating Rita* (Chester Gateway).

Musical Theatre includes *The Pirates of Penzance* (Gielgud Theatre), *Fiddler on the Roof* (Savoy Theatre and Sheffield Crucible), *Into The Woods* (Royal Opera House), *How to Succeed in Business Without Really Trying, Six Pictures of Lee Miller* (Chichester Festival Company), *Jerry Springer The Opera* (Edinburgh Festival), *Sweeney Todd* (Opera North), *Candide, Honk the Ugly Duckling* (National Theatre), *Night After Night* (Royal Court), *Company* (Manchester Library Theatre), *Les Miserables* (RSC and Palace Theatre), *Happy End* (Nottingham Playhouse), *Carousel* (Royal Exchange Theatre) and *A Little Night Music* (Ipswich).

Opera includes *Arms and the Cow* (Opera North), *HMS Pinafore, Die Fledermaus, The Pirates of Penzance* (Carl Rosa) and *The Magic Flute* (Music Theatre London).

Television includes *Doctors, Casualty, Gimme Gimme Gimme, The Hello Girls* and *Paris*.

Celia Meiras Nelly

Theatre includes *Senora Carrar's Rifle* (Young Vic), *Not the End of the World, Alice's Adventures in Wonderland* (Bristol Old Vic), *That Pesky Rat, an Oak Tree* (Soho Theatre), *The Odyssey* (Lyric Hammersmith), *Nathan the Wise, In Arabia we'd all be Kings* (Hampstead Theatre), *Julius Caesar* (Barbican, BITE and International tour), *Charley's Aunt* (The Northcott Exeter), *The Dice House* (The Arts Theatre), *Hannah and Hanna* (BAC, The Arcola, Edinburgh Festival, Indian Tour), *Merlin the Magnificent* (Regent's Park) and *Caledonian Rd* (The Almeida).

Television and film includes *I Could Never Be Your Woman, Dot The I, Va'nunu, One Summer's day, Nathan Barley, Doctors, Silent Witness, Eastenders* and *Extra Espanol*.

Radio includes *Captain Corelli's Mandolin, Darling Alicia, I wish I could turn and live with Animals* (Radio 4) *Hannah and Hanna* (BBC World Service).

Company

Wajdi Mouawad *Writer*

Born in Lebanon in 1968, Wajdi Mouawad fled the country with his family; they lived in Paris for a few years, then settled in Montreal. In 1991, shortly after graduating from the National Theatre School, he embarked on a quadruple career as an actor, writer, director and producer.

In January 2002, the government of France named Wajdi Mouawad a Chevalier de l'Ordre National des Arts et des Lettres in recognition of his lifetime artistic contribution. He is the recipient of numerous awards and honours for his writing. Mouawad is a totally original voice in Québécois theatre, spanning the cultural gaps that can exist between his native Lebanon, North America, Québec and Europe.

Shelley Tepperman *Translator*

Shelley Tepperman has a long history in Canadian theatre specialising in new play dramaturgy, project development and translation for the stage. Her many translations from French, Spanish and Italian have been produced at CBC radio and on stages across North America, and she has twice been a finalist for the Governor General's Literary award. She has translated three other plays by Wajdi Mouawad: *Alphonse*, *Littoral* (*Tideline*) and *Pacamambo*. Shelley has worked for CBC Radio developing, adapting and directing/producing radio dramas for national broadcast and also works in documentary film and television as a writer, story editor and director.

Patricia Benecke *Director*

Patricia is joint Artistic Director of Dialogue Productions. For them she has directed *Helter Skelter/Land of the Dead*, *Monsieur Ibrahim and the Flowers of the Qur'an*, *Top Dogs*, *Merlin*, *Heroes Like Us* and *The MC of a Striptease Act Doesn't Give Up*.

Patricia works as a director in the UK and Germany. Previous repertory work includes *Miss Julie* (Mercury Theatre), *By the Bog of Cats* (Heilbronn Rep), *Shining City* (Dortmund Rep) and *Realism* (Bonn Rep). Future work includes *A Midsummer Night's Dream* (Potsdam Rep), *Woman and Scarecrow* (Dortmund) and *The Miser* (Bonn).

She is associate director at the Horizont Theatre, Cologne, where her directing work includes: *Ghosts*, *Twilight of the Golds*, *The Fireraisers*, *The Transformed Comedian* and *Far Away* (nominated for the Cologne Theatre Award).

Patricia is also a translator and the British theatre correspondent for Theater Heute and Neue Zürcher Zeitung.

Sara Perks *Designer*

Theatre credits include *Helter Skelter/Land of The Dead* (The Bush Theatre), *Treasure Island* (Derby Playhouse), *Rough For Theatre 1 & 2* (Arts Theatre, London), *Return To The Forbidden Planet* (national tour), *Dead Funny* (Oldham and national tour), *Romeo and Juliet* (English Touring Theatre, national tour and Hong Kong Arts Festival), *The Crypt Project* (St Andrews

Crypt London, Sincera Productions), *The Elixir of Love* (Grange Park Opera, co-design), *Journey's End*, *Julius Caesar*, *Coriolanus*, *Miss Julie*, *The Importance of Being Earnest*, *The Seagull*, *Twelfth Night*, *To Kill A Mockingbird*, *Macbeth*, *Private Lives* and *The Caucasian Chalk Circle* (all Mercury Theatre, Colchester), *Death of A Salesman* (Colchester and Ipswich), *Skylight*, *Be My Baby* (Dukes, Lancaster), *The Deep Blue Sea*, *The Ladykillers*, *Dancing at Lughnasa*, *As You Like It*, *Romeo and Juliet*, *Habeas Corpus* (Northcott, Exeter), *Reunion* and *Dark Pony* (Kings Head, London), *Much Ado About Nothing*, *Romeo and Juliet*, *Merchant of Venice*, *Hamlet* and *Arabian Nights* (various site-specific venues for Creation in Oxford, including Oxford Castle and the Spiegel Tent), *Aeroplane Bones*, *Gringos*, *The Bald Prima Donna* (Bristol Old Vic and BAC), Belle (The Gate, London), *Frankie and Tommy* (Lyric, Hammersmith), *Union Street*, *Monkey!* and *The Lost Domain* (Theatre Royal and Drum, Plymouth), *The Old Curiosity Shop* (Southwark Playhouse) and the original and several subsequent production of the cult musical *Saucy Jack and The Space Vixens* (most recently in its own nightclub in the London Bridge vaults).

Awards include the BBC Vision Design, John Elvery Theatre Design Award and an Edinburgh Fringe First.

Hansjörg Schmidt
Lighting Designer

Recent theatre in London: *Under Glass* (clod ensemble), *Camera Obscura* and *Going Off* (BAC), *Helen Of Troy* and *The Caucasian*

Chalk Circle (Steam Industry at The Scoop), *The Taming of the Shrew* and *Performances* (Wilton's Music Hall), *The Next Big Thing* (West End), *Saucy Jack and the Space Vixens* (West End), *The Rat Trap* and *Loyalties* (Finborough), *The Death of Gogol and the 1969 Eurovision Song Contest* (Drill Hall), *Misery* (Kings Head).

Regional and touring: *Coriolanus*, *Julius Caesar* (both at the Mercury Theatre Colchester), *Blue Orange* (New Vic Theatre) *A Midsummer Night's Dream* (KAOS Theatre), *Northanger Abbey* (Salisbury Playhouse and on tour), *Red Ladies* (clod ensemble), *Much Ado About Nothing*, *Billy Liar*, *Around the World in 80 Days* (Liverpool Playhouse), *The Dreaming Place* (fevered sleep at The Egg, Theatre Royal Bath), *Hospitalworks* (theatre-rites, London and Theater der Welt, Stuttgart), *Master Harold...and the boys* (Liverpool Everyman), *A Perfect Ganesh* (Watford Palace), *Pal Joey* (Nottingham Playhouse).

Other projects: *Christmas Lights*, a architectural lighting installation at Goldsmiths College University of London, *Jessica Ogden Collection SS06*, for London Fashion Week at Sunbeam Studios, *The Beautiful Octopus Club* and *Unplugged*, for Heart 'n Soul at the Deptford Albany and on tour.

Nikola Kodjabashia
Music & Sound

Nikola is a lecturer in Creative Music Technology at DeepBlueSound Studios for Plymouth City College and in Music Composition for Media at Plymouth College of Art & Design.

Theatre credits include *Helter Skelter/Land of the Dead*, *Monsieur*

Ibrahim and the Flowers of the Qur'an (Bush Theatre), *Hecuba* (Donmar Warehouse), *The Birds,* and *The Bacchae* (National Theatre).

Television and film credits include *Racism, A History, Saints, Green Pages, The Great Water, Remain Upstanding,* and *Dust*.

Nikola has been awarded the British Council Chevening Award and created an Orchestral Commission for the Venice Biennale 2004.

Susannah Pack
Assistant Director

Theatre credits as director include:

Ca$h in Christ (World Premiere, Assembly Rooms, Edinburgh), *Best Friends* (UK Premiere, New End Theatre, Fringe First Nomination at Edinburgh Festival), Hanif Kureishi's *Intimacy* (World Premiere, Assembly Rooms, Edinburgh; Bath Theatre Royal; Bull Theatre, Barnet), *Gathering of Birds* (World Premiere, C Venues, Edinburgh), *My Night With Reg* (MAC, Birmingham; C Venues, Edinburgh) and numerous rehearsed readings, including *Consider This* (Soho Theatre) and *Return, Little Mercury, Return* (Barons Court Theatre).

Credits as assistant director include:

For Dialogue Productions, *Helter Skelter / Land Of The Dead* (Bush Theatre).

Also *Underneath The Lintel* (Duchess Theatre), *The Odd Couple* (Assembly Hall, Edinburgh), *Taking Charlie, Oleanna, Resolution* (Assembly Rooms, Edinburgh & National Tours). She is Artistic Director of the award-winning company Wisepart Productions, for which she has directed and produced several shows that have toured nationally and internationally. Susannah has been selected for numerous programmes, including the National Theatre Studio Director's Programme and the TIF Producer's Course.

DIALOGUE PRODUCTIONS

Dialogue Productions was founded in 1996 with the aim of enhancing cultural dialogue between Great Britain and Germany by premiering the best contemporary German speaking drama in England. Subsequent projects have extended the company remit to wider international work.

Key personnel are German director Patricia Benecke and British actor Patrick Driver.

Company patrons are Max Stafford-Clark, Christoph Marthaler and Nadim Sawalha.

Productions to date:

2008: British premiere of *Helter Skelter/Land of the Dead* by Neil LaBute at The Bush Theatre

2006: British premiere of *Monsieur Ibrahim and the Flowers of the Qur'an* by Eric-Emmanuel Schmitt at The Bush Theatre, Assembly Rooms (Edinburgh Festival) and on national tour

2005: National tour of Urs Widmer's *Top Dogs*

2003: *Top Dogs* revival at Southwark Playhouse

2001: Tankred Dorst's *Merlin*, the English premiere of this modern German classic, at the Riverside Studios Mainhouse

2000: British premiere of Thomas Brussig's *Heroes like Us*, in association with NXT, at The Edinburgh Festival

1998: British premiere of Urs Widmer's *Top Dogs*, presented as a site specific performance at The Truman Brewery in Brick Lane

1996–2003: British premiere of Bodo Kirchhoff's *The MC of a Striptease Act Doesn't Give Up*, staged in London, Germany, Holland, Italy, Ireland, USA and at the Edinburgh Festival

This production of *Wedding Day at the Cro-Magnons'* was made possible by the generous support of Fondation Maurice & Noémie de Rothschild.

It is also supported by Québec Government Office, London.

www.dialogueproductions.co.uk

mercurytheatre
(COLCHESTER)

The Mercury Theatre Colchester is unique in having a highly respected ensemble company producing classic plays as well as working extensively in the community. It has been successful since its inception in 1999, being described by the Daily Telegraph as *"a hive of artistic excellence"* and by the Guardian as *"one of the best small reps in the country."* In autumn 2007, the Mercury Theatre Company presented a Shakespeare season featuring an all male production of *Coriolanus* and all female production of *Julius Caesar*.

Since 2003, The Company has built up a strong reputation and audience for new writing. Producing *Slammers I* and *II* in successive years (three shots of invigorating new theatre written, directed and performed by company members), has led onto productions including *Brass Balls* and *Small Miracle*, (transferred to The Tricycle in summer 2007), also written by company actors and performed to critical acclaim.

Other Mercury Theatre Company new writing productions include Jonathan Lichtenstein's *The Pull of Negative Gravity*, (Edinburgh Festival 2005 and New York's 59E59 2006) winner of a Fringe First Award and nationally acclaimed by the broadsheets; *Devils Advocate* (Edinburgh Festival 2006 *"Among the very best acting in Edinburgh this summer"* Daily Telegraph and PENN winner for Playwright Donald Freed); the world premiere of Donald Freed's *The White Crow*; and *Blue Sky State* by Anna Reynolds.

Amongst others, the Mercury collaborates with Dialogue Productions, Real Circumstance, Tilted Productions, The New Wolsey Theatre and Wildworks, with whom performances of *Souterrain* took place in a disused department store in Colchester as well as site-specific locations across Europe.

With a number of exciting projects in the pipeline, in 2008 the Mercury continues to get strong new writing in front of audiences by producing with Dialogue Productions and Soho Theatre for this production of *Wedding Day at the Cro-Magnons'* and with Scamp Theatre for *Charlie Victor Romeo* at the Mercury Theatre and Edinburgh Festival.

● soho theatre

performance	provocative and compelling theatre, comedy and cabaret
talks	vibrant debates on culture, the arts and the way we live
soho connect	a thriving education, community and outreach programme
writers' centre	discovering and nurturing new writers and artists
soho theatre bar	serving tasty, affordable food and drink from 12pm till late

'The capital's centre for daring international drama.' Evening Standard
'London's coolest theatre by a mile' Midweek

21 Dean Street
London W1D 3NE
Admin: 020 7287 5060
Box Office: 0870 429 6883
sohotheatre.com

Soho Theatre online
Giving you the latest information and previews of upcoming shows, Soho Theatre can be found on facebook, myspace and youtube as well as at sohotheatre.com

For regular programme updates and offers visit sohotheatre.com/mailing

Hiring the theatre
Soho Theatre has a range of rooms and spaces for hire. Please contact the theatre on 020 7287 5060 or go to sohotheatre.com/hires for further details.

Suspect Culture & Graeae Theatre Company
in association with the Tron Theatre, Glasgow present

STATIC

Script Dan Rebellato | Direction Graham Eatough & Jenny Sealey
Design Ian Scott | Sound Kenny MacLeod
A story of love, loss and compilation tapes.

'A compelling evening's theatre'
Edinburgh Evening News

'A contemporary, touching discussion of music as a life, as communication, as everything'
British Theatre Guide

at Soho Theatre 22 April – 10 May, 7.30pm

THE SOHO THEATRE DEVELOPMENT CAMPAIGN

Soho Theatre receives core funding from Arts Council England, London.

In order to provide as diverse a programme as possible and expand our audience development and outreach work, we rely upon additional support from trusts, foundations, individuals and businesses. All of our major sponsors share a common commitment to developing new areas of activity and encouraging creative partnerships between business and the arts. We are immensely grateful for the invaluable support from our sponsors and donors and wish to thank them for their continued commitment.

Soho Theatre has a Friends Scheme in support of its education programme and work developing new writers and reaching new audiences. To find out how to become a Friend of Soho Theatre, contact the development department on 020 7478 0109, email development@sohotheatre.com or visit sohotheatre.com.

Sponsors:
Angels, The Costumiers, Bloomberg, Rathbones, TEQUILA\London

Principal Supporters and Education Patrons:
Anonymous
The City Bridge Trust
The Ernest Cook Trust
Tony and Rita Gallagher
Nigel Gee
The Paul Hamlyn Foundation
Roger Jospé
Jack and Linda Keenan
John Lyon's Charity
Man Group plc Charitable Trust
Sigrid Rausing
The Rose Foundation
Diana Toeman
Carolyn Ward
The Harold Hyam Wingate Foundation

Soho Supporting Partner:
Goodman Derrick

Soho Business Members:
The Groucho Club
Ronnie Scott's Jazz Club

Trusts and Foundations:
Anonymous
The Carr-Gregory Trust
Miss Hazel Wood Charitable Trust
Hyde Park Place Estate Charity

The Kobler Trust
The Mackintosh Foundation
Teale Charitable Trust

Belarus Free Theatre Campaign:
Anonymous
Anglo-Belarusian Society
Alan Bennett
Caryl Churchill
Count Andrew Ciechanowiecki
Richard Curtis
Michael Frayn
Jenny Hall
David Heyman
Nicholas Hytner
Emma Thompson
Alan Rickman

Dear Friends:
Anonymous
Jill and Michael Barrington
David Day
John Drummond
Madeleine Hamel
Norma Heyman
Jane and Andrew McManus
Michael and Mimi Naughton
Hannah Pierce
Nicola Stanhope
Alex Vogel

Good Friends and Friends:
Thank you also to the many Soho Friends we are unable to list here.

For a full list of our patrons, please visit sohotheatre.com

Registered Charity: 267234

WEDDING DAY AT THE CRO-MAGNONS'

Journée de noces chez les Cro-Magnons © 2001, Leméac Éditeur (Montreal, Canada)

Wedding Day at the Cro-Magnons' first published in 2002 by Playwrights Canada Press

First published in this edition in 2008 by Oberon Books Ltd
521 Caledonian Road, London N7 9RH
Tel: 020 7607 3637 / Fax: 020 7607 3629
e-mail: info@oberonbooks.com
www.oberonbooks.com

A catalogue record for this book is available from the British Library.

PB ISBN: 9781840028485
E ISBN: 9781786823830

Cover design by Jane Harper (photography by Robert Asser)

Printed and bound by Marston Book Services, Didcot.
eBook conversion by Lapiz Digital Services, India.

Characters

NEYIF – the father, 50s

NAZHA – the mother, 50s

NELLY – the daughter, 30

NEEL – the younger son, 17

SOUHAYLA – the neighbour, about 35

THE GENTLEMAN – early 30s

HISTORY OF THE ENGLISH VERSION

Journée de noces chez les Cro-Magnons premiered at Montreal's Théâtre d'Aujourd'hui in January 1993. The English version was co-produced in Canada by Toronto's Theatre Passe Muraille and the National Arts Centre in Ottawa in 1996. That production was directed by Banuta Rubess, and in the process the original five-act play was adapted to a four-act version.

This version of the play reflects cuts made by Dialogue Productions. North American words and expressions were replaced by British equivalents by Patricia Benecke, Patrick Driver and the cast.

Anyone wishing to obtain the North American script or the full five-act version should contact:
Agence Simard Denoncourt,
4305 d'Iberville, Bureau 101 Montreal, Canada H2H 2L5
(514-843.2024 aasd@qc.aira.com).

Act One

A middle class apartment, visibly damaged by bombing. Morning.

NAZHA: That's not how it's going to start this time!

NEEL: It always starts the same way, Mama!

NAZHA: Shit!

NEEL: How else do you want it to start if not the same way?!

NAZHA: What is this rubbish?!

NEEL: Always, always, always the same way!

NAZHA: Who chose the lettuce – you or the Armenian?!

NEEL: Mama!

NAZHA: Was it you or that monkey turd who chose this lettuce, Neel?!

NEEL: It was him!

NAZHA: Just look at this! Stick your nose in it!

NEEL: Don't get so UPSET!

NAZHA: And now explain to me how on earth, I mean, what brilliant technique am I supposed to use to turn shit like this into food!

NEEL: Alright! Don't get so upset about a fucking lettuce!

NAZHA: What are you doing?!

NEEL: I'll go to the Greek this time!

NAZHA: Oh, brilliant. My son is an ass. I have an ass for a son!

NEEL: And if I don't find any lettuce at the Greek's, I'll steal some from the sheikh's garden!

NAZHA: Where the hell do you think you're going?!

NEEL: To the Greek to get your fucking lettuce!

NAZHA: Great. And afterwards, I'll just drag our neighbours to your funeral! I can just see the look on their faces…Don't you dare leave this house!

NEEL: Well it's pretty stupid to do this on a day they're bombing!

NAZHA: How could we have known? We couldn't have guessed! You can't predict idiocy like you can predict the weather!

NEEL: Yes well, weather's not exactly rosy is it; look over there, the sky is growling at us; soon it'll be all black!

NAZHA: Fine. Your sister's dress will look all the more white!

NEEL: My sister's dress is still at the dressmaker's!

NAZHA: He's going to bring it over before noon.

NEEL: If he doesn't get blown up on the way!

NAZHA: (*Returning to her lettuce.*) Ugh, he wiped himself with it!

NEEL: Sunshine all day, they said. Don't make me laugh!

NAZHA: He wipes his arse with his lettuces, that disgusting slob! Don't ever go back to the Armenian's, do you hear me?!

NEEL: We'll never go back to the Armenian's.

NAZHA: He sells lettuce that smells of fish.

NEEL: What do you have against fish?

NAZHA: Bring me a bag and throw out this crap. We're not having salad.

NEEL: No salad.

NAZHA: Right, no salad. You don't need salad for a meal, my boy. Come to think of it, it's better not to have salad.

NEEL: I told you it'll always start the same way. Always, always, always.

NAZHA: You think so? No!

No! If there isn't any salad, we'll have potatoes. I know, we'll fry them! Yes, that's it. We'll have fried potatoes! Get me the cloth bag under the kitchen sink, I think I still have some good potatoes left. No one's going to tell me there won't be a wedding feast the day of my daughter's wedding. We'll have potatoes.

NEEL: Those potatoes are rotten, Mama!

NAZHA: Well, all the more reason to use them up! We can't be throwing out food when there are men fighting just a hundred yards away. No, we're going to fry those potatoes.

NEEL: If the potatoes are friable, we'll bloody well fry them.

NAZHA: Come on, don't dawdle, we'll have to skin them.

NEEL: If the potatoes are skinnable, we'll bloody well skin them.

NAZHA: Fucking shit! With all this, I still haven't finished.

NELLY: (*Off.*) When are we going to Berdawnay? Next Friday?

NAZHA: Not again!

NEEL: That's the third time in two hours.

NELLY: (*Off.*) When are we going to Berdawnay?

NEEL: Next Friday!

NAZHA: She must have fallen asleep under the sink again. Go and get her.

NEEL: And Walter?

NAZHA: Walter didn't sleep at home last night.

NEEL: Again?

NAZHA: As usual.

NEEL: But he promised he'd come home and play with me.

SOUHAYLA knocks and enters carrying several delicious looking plates of food. In the distance, light bombing is heard.

SOUHAYLA: At last!

NAZHA: Souhayla!

NEEL: He promised me!

SOUHAYLA: I thought I'd give you a hand!

NAZHA: You're such a darling, Souhayla!

NELLY: (*Off.*) When are we going to Berdawnay?

SOUHAYLA puts the dishes down.

NEEL: Next Friday! He promised he'd come and play with me.

NAZHA: But you shouldn't have! No, really, you shouldn't
have. It's too much! It's really too much! Ya aybeyshoom!
Really, ya aybeyshoom! Why did you go to so much
trouble! My goodness!

SOUHAYLA: The women and I decided to make you a few
little dishes.

NELLY: (*Off.*) Next Friday?

NEEL: Next Friday.

SOUHAYLA: They're all going to come, you know.

NAZHA: They're all going to come?

SOUHAYLA: All of them! With their husbands and daughters.

NELLY: (*Off.*) Next Friday?

NEEL: He promised me!

NAZHA: Stop it Neel!

NEEL: Yes, but he promised me!

NAZHA: He promised, he promised…he always promises.

NELLY: (*Off.*) Next Friday?

NAZHA: And go and check on your sister! Excuse me, my dear
Souhayla! This is all so embarrassing. My God! Fassoulia!
And Tabbouleh! Go and see your sister, Neel. And a plate
of Keshk – and Kibbeh, of course. Oh, don't they smell
delicious! What an aroma!

SOUHAYLA: The neighbours are very happy for your daughter! They all told me! They're going to wear their prettiest dresses.

NAZHA: It's going to be an incredible party. The bombs will freeze in the sky!

NEEL: But I bet the rain won't!

NAZHA: Ya aybeyshoom! All the work I was expected to do. Really, it's too much. It's too much!

NEEL: I'll go and get the potatoes.

NAZHA: (*To NEEL.*) Make the coffee while you're in there! What a delicious smell!

NEEL has left.

SOUHAYLA: Is he alright? He seems a bit nervous these days.

NAZHA: Oh! Poor thing. Maybe one day things will sort themselves out in that poor head of his. I don't know… We can only hope…

SOUHAYLA: It can't be very easy for you!

NAZHA: Don't ask! We can't even send him to school. The situation is just too volatile!

SOUHAYLA: All the women understand. We all talk about it!

NAZHA: I know. He should never have been born!

NELLY: (*Off.*) Next Friday we're going to Berdawnay?

NEEL: (*Off.*) That's right, next Friday, we're going to Berdawnay.

NAZHA: You know he can only bear the sound of the bombing when he's inside the house.

SOUHAYLA: Unbelievable! Is he really that sensitive?

NELLY: (*Off.*) Are we going to eat kneffay?

NEEL: (*Off.*) We're going to stuff our faces with it!

NAZHA: His father and I don't know how to help him get used to the bombing. Maybe he'll learn to enjoy it.

SOUHAYLA: Poor boy! Poor Neel!

NEEL: (*Off.*) Mama, your potatoes are off! They stink!

NAZHA: We don't have any choice, Neel. If you want you can come and peel them here!

NELLY: (*Off.*) When are we going to Berdawnay to eat kneffay?

NEEL: (*Off.*) Next Friday!

NELLY: (*Off.*) Next Friday we're going to Berdawnay to eat kneffay?

NEEL: (*Off.*) Yes!

NELLY: (*Off.*) Next Friday?

NEEL: (*Off.*) Next Friday.

NELLY: (*Off.*) When are we going to Berdawnay?

NEEL: (*Off.*) Next Friday!

NELLY: (*Off.*) Next Friday we're going to Berdawnay to eat kneffay?

NEEL: (*Off.*) Yes!

NELLY: (*Off.*) When are we going to Berdawnay to eat kneffay? Next Friday?

NEEL: (*Off, shouting.*) Yeeessssss!

NAZHA: Oh, but the fiancé, my dear Souhayla, just you wait…the fiancé! The fiancé, Souhayla…he's the kind of…he's so…Ah! He's a man full of…charm, yes! Charm, my dear! Charm!

NEEL: (*Entering with a pot of Turkish coffee.*) I'm fed up! I'm fed up! I'm completely fed up!!!

NAZHA: Stop whining, Neel.

NEEL: She doesn't want to wake up!

NAZHA: Be careful, Neel! Darling you're spilling coffee everywhere! Here you go, my dear Souhayla.

SOUHAYLA: So...the fiancé?

NAZHA: He's so charming, my dear, he's unbelievably charming. Did you know he bought a car for the occasion?

SOUHAYLA: A car!

NAZHA: Yes, my dear! A car! From Europe!

NELLY: (*Off.*) What's new?

NEEL: Everything's old.

NELLY: (*Off.*) What's new?

NEEL: Everything's old.

NELLY: (*Off.*) Everything's old?

NEEL: Everything's old!

NELLY: (*Off.*) When are we going to Berdawnay to eat kneffay?

NEEL: Next Friday!

NAZHA: A beautiful car, yes! We weren't going to give our little girl away to just anyone!

SOUHAYLA: With the war it isn't easy to find somebody suitable in this country.

NAZHA: Ah yes! We said – her father and I – that since it's impossible in a situation like ours to give our children a decent education, we might as well give them, yes give them away, to someone who's had the time, that's it, the time! Who's had the time to go to school, to study, to become somebody!

SOUHAYLA: That's exactly it! To become somebody. To be somebody.

NAZHA: Hey, in this country, nobody is a somebody anymore!

SOUHAYLA: Basically, there's nobody left in this country!

NELLY: (*Off.*) Next Friday we're going to Berdawnay?

23

NEEL: Fucking hell!

NAZHA: Neel!

NEEL: I'd like to fall asleep all of a sudden all over the place as well!

NAZHA: Stop it!

NEEL: And your potatoes are not peelable!

NAZHA: Stop shouting, do you mind!

NEEL: They're NOT PEELABLE!

NAZHA: (*Placating.*) Yes they are, they are, sweetie, they are.

NEEL: The minute I get hold of them, they fall apart in my hands!

NAZHA: You're squeezing them too hard!

NEEL: I'm hardly touching them!

NAZHA: Here! Look! You have to hold them gently! Go on! We'll tell everyone that you peeled them!

SOUHAYLA: You're serving potatoes at your daughter's wedding?

NAZHA and NEEL speak the following two portions of dialogue simultaneously.

NAZHA: They're to go with the mutton! To go with the leg. The leg of mutton.

NEEL: In a toss up between potatoes and lettuce that smells like fish, I wouldn't think twice…

NAZHA: We're having a leg of mutton! And to go with the leg of mutton, we're going to fry some potatoes.

NEEL: I'd have gone for the fish! At least the fish was fresh!

SOUHAYLA: Well, I brought you a little something! Now, it's nothing much…

NAZHA: What is it?

SOUHAYLA: Open it up and have a look!

NAZHA: You shouldn't have! You really shouldn't have! Souhayla! Ya aybeyshoom! Really! Ya aybeyshoom! Ooooh! Beyleywa! You must be insane! This is far too extravagant!

SOUHAYLA: For a wedding, my dear Nazha, nothing's too extravagant!

NEEL: Shitty pukeworthy potato mush!

NAZHA: Neel! You're starting to get on my nerves! I'd like to drink my coffee in peace.

NEEL: I'm pissed off! I'm a little boy in the prime of youth and my life shouldn't be about peeling unpeelable potatoes! I should be outside playing with my friends! I want to play outside with my friends!

NAZHA: You can't! There are too many snipers.

NEEL: Where's Walter?

A violent explosion, fairly close by.

SOUHAYLA: My God, what a storm! Nature's certainly very powerful!

NEEL: That's not a storm! That was a 255 that just exploded in the south quarter.

NAZHA: If only it were a storm! It might calm everybody down!

NEEL: I'm sick to death of potatoes that stink of war. They give me a pain in the balls. I can't peel them. They're all soft and they fall apart in my hands.

NAZHA: All right! All right! Stop shouting!

NEEL: I'm sick to death of this dump! I'm sick to death of this wedding! It gives me a pain in the gonads! One more putrid potato and they're gonna burst!

NAZHA: That's enough! Stop peeling the potatoes! You're right, they're not peelable!

NEEL: They're rotten!

NAZHA: You're right, the potatoes are rotten! And they fall apart in your hands!

NEEL: Fucking right!

NAZHA: That's enough! We'll make mashed potatoes! We'll serve them mashed! Go and put them in the mixer!

SOUHAYLA: Is there anything I can do?

NAZHA: Oh no, my dear Souhayla! Ya aybeyshoom! You're here to brighten up my morning by having a little coffee with me! Anyway, there's really nothing I can do until Neyif gets back from the slaughterhouse. He's gone to get the mutton.

SOUHAYLA: But surely there are other things to be done…

NEEL: Tickle my bum.

SOUHAYLA: What can I help to prepare?

NEEL: Tickle my hair.

NAZHA: Well, I have to scoop out the battenjen and the coussa. Maybe I still have some eggs…

NEEL: Tickle my legs.

SOUHAYLA: Well then! Let's get to work on the coussa and the battenjen. Do you have a towel?

NEEL: Tickle my bowel.

NAZHA: Neel!

NEEL: You can't even have fun around here anymore!

NAZHA: (*To NEEL.*) Get me the paper bag on the kitchen counter!

NEEL: When I think that right now, in America, black men ten feet tall are playing basketball…!

NEEL exits.

SOUHAYLA: Don't get upset, my dear. His brother's absence must be so difficult for him. You have to understand him.

NAZHA: I do understand him! I do understand him! It's just that I'm starting to lose my fucking patience!

NELLY: (*Off.*) Mama.

NAZHA: (*To SOUHAYLA.*) She's awake! (*To NELLY.*) Yes, darling?

NELLY: (*Off.*) Is my dress here yet?

NAZHA: Not yet, sweetheart. The fiancé, Souhayla, he's...he's very...virile!

SOUHAYLA: Ahhhh!

NAZHA: He's tall, he's strong, he's noble, he's handsome!

SOUHAYLA: Ohhhh!

NAZHA: And people say he's very clever! Yes! Cultured! That he's rich, and that he can walk right into a career in a skyscraper!

NEEL enters with several aubergines and courgettes.

NEEL: Here's the coussa and the battenjen. Now I get to magimix the potatoes.

NELLY: (*Off.*) Mama.

NAZHA: Yes, darling?

NELLY: (*Off.*) Who's there?

NAZHA: Souhayla.

NELLY: (*Off.*) Hello Souhayla.

SOUHAYLA: Oh! Nelly! I'm so happy! I'm so happy! I am so happy!

NEEL: There you go: she's very happy and we're absolutely thrilled for her.

A very violent clap of thunder.

SOUHAYLA: Oh my God! What on earth is that!

NEEL: It's the storm, calm down! Calm down!

NAZHA: It was awfully close!

SOUHAYLA: You're sure it was only the storm?

NEEL: I can tell the difference between the storm and a 255 or even a 590!

NELLY: (*Off.*) When are we going to Berdawnay?

NEEL: Next Friday.

NAZHA: She's falling asleep again.

NEEL: It can only start the same way, I'm telling you!

NAZHA places her coffee cup upside down on the table. SOUHAYLA follows suit.

NAZHA: Let's start scooping, my dear, let's start scooping, that's all we have left to do!

SOUHAYLA: We have to hurry, the morning's almost over! What time is the fiancé arriving?

NAZHA: At 4:00, like all fiancés.

NELLY: (*Off.*) We're going to eat kneffay?

NEEL: (*To NELLY.*) We're going to eat kneffay. (*To NAZHA.*) It's starting to rain, see, it really was the storm!

SOUHAYLA: The battenjen is lovely!

NAZHA: Isn't it!

SOUHAYLA: Is it from the Armenian's?

NAZHA: No, my dear! It's from the Greek's – at least HE watches where he puts HIS vegetables!

SOUHAYLA: People say the Armenian is vulgar –

NAZHA: He is vulgar, my dear, he is! And his dog! That maggot-ridden mutt! Good God. Always prancing all over the shop. All you can see is a swarm of flies around a rotting carcass! That dog makes me want to puke! There is nothing more repulsive than that drooling shit-encrusted fleabag!

NEEL turns on the mixer. The noise is monstrous.

NAZHA / SOUHAYLA: Ahhh! What on earth is that?

NEEL: The mixer!

SOUHAYLA: It's the mixer!

NAZHA: Neel!

SOUHAYLA: He can't hear you!

NEEL: Mama…

NAZHA: What?

SOUHAYLA: What?

NAZHA: I said: what did you say?

SOUHAYLA: I said he can't hear you!

NEEL: Mama! Mama! I can't make it stop!

NAZHA: I'll unplug it.

SOUHAYLA: What?

NEEL: I don't know how to stop it, I don't know how to stop it, I don't know –

NAZHA unplugs the mixer.

NAZHA: At last! What a relief!

SOUHAYLA: Silence at last!

NEEL: Don't shout at me, Mama! I – I – I don't know what I'd do if you shouted at me, Mama! Maybe throw myself against the wall or even – out of the window! Yes, out of the window if you shouted at me, Mama!

NAZHA: But…!

NEEL: Mama! I love you! This fucking war! My mother is dead and it isn't a dream!

NAZHA: Neel, sweetheart! My baby! Don't be silly! It's not your fault that the mixer doesn't work! And why did you say I'm dead, you fool?

NEEL: Where's Walter who still isn't here?

NAZHA: Why did you say I was dead?

NEEL: And where's Papa?

NAZHA: Papa will be here, soon! You know what your father's like, he hates getting wet! So he must be staying dry somewhere!

NEEL: With the leg of mutton?

NAZHA: Yes! Yes, darling, with the leg of mutton!

NEEL: And he'll be here soon?

NAZHA: Yes. Soon. Alright! Now, we have work to do!

SOUHAYLA: The battenjen, and the coussa! Because, after all, it's a special day today! You really have to do this in style! It isn't everyday that you give away your only daughter!

NAZHA: No, it's not!…it isn't every day you give away your only daughter!

SOUHAYLA: What is our sleeping beauty doing?

NEEL: She's taking a bath!

SOUHAYLA: Does she still drop off to sleep as often?

NAZHA: Oh yes!!

SOUHAYLA: Poor Nelly! This slumber that descends on her without warning, wherever she happens to be!

NAZHA: In a war-torn country narcolepsy is a gift from God!

NEEL: You can say that again!

NAZHA: Oh! The potatoes! Go and mash them by hand.

NEEL: (*Exiting.*) This is really gross!

NAZHA: The coffee grounds must be ready by now! Let's see what they reveal!

SOUHAYLA: Nazha! We don't have time to waste on silly games.

NAZHA: We have time! We have time!

NEEL: (*Returning, singing softly.*) Sleeping Beauty, lily white, tiptoed through the piercing night!

NAZHA looks closely at the cup of coffee, turning it. She studies it in an unsettling silence.

SOUHAYLA is on tenterhooks.

NAZHA: I see a man!…A young man. Young and strong.

SOUHAYLA: The same one as last time??

NAZHA: I think so…! Yes, there he is – the same one as last time. He's waiting. Standing by the gate. He seems to be waiting for something. I don't know what.

NEEL: He's waiting for death. Any man waiting in this country, especially if he's young and strong, won't stay alive very long.

NAZHA: Beside him is a white cock crowing into the sunset… he doesn't seem to notice the young man who doesn't move an inch!

NEEL: How could he move an inch inside that coffee cup!

SOUHAYLA: This young man…what does he look like?

NAZHA: Long black hair…and he's very strong! He's wearing tight trousers and his shirt is unbuttoned to the navel. He's waiting!

NEEL: One day I swear you'll read potatoes and see my face…

NEEL exits with the dish of potatoes.

NAZHA: You don't know anyone young and strong with long black hair who wears tight trousers??

SOUHAYLA: Yes, my father! But he isn't young and he never wears tight trousers, he says they give him a rash.

NAZHA: What can I tell you? Mark my words, my dear Souhayla, you'll be married before Christmas.

SOUHAYLA: Before Christmas?

NAZHA: Before Christmas!

SOUHAYLA: Let's hope so. From your mouth to God's ear. (*A beat.*) Actually, it's a bit cold before Christmas.

NELLY: (*Off.*) We're going to Berdawnay next Friday?

NEEL: (*Off.*) Yes!

SOUHAYLA: I'd rather wait until May.

NAZHA: Let's get started on the hummus. Neel! Go and get the hummus! Oh my God! The mutton! Neyif isn't back yet! With snipers all over the place! Let's hope nothing's happened to him! (*To NEEL.*) Get a plate for the beyleywa, too.

NELLY: (*Off, a horrified shriek.*) Mama!

SOUHAYLA: My God! What's the matter with Nelly?

NAZHA: She must be dreaming and calling me in her sleep!

NEEL: (*Off.*) Mama! Nelly just fell down all naked under the sink!

SOUHAYLA: Oh my God!

NELLY: (*Off.*) Mama!

NAZHA: She must be having a nightmare!

NAZHA exits, NEEL enters.

NEEL: Poor Mama! It's amazing she's still so lucid!

SOUHAYLA: Neel! That isn't very nice!

NEEL: So tell me, Souhayla, what are you doing here today? What on earth compels you to witness this pathetic farce?

SOUHAYLA: What farce Neel?

NEEL: How can you be so dense?!

SOUHAYLA: You're really out of order today! You're in one of those moods that upset your mother. Why are you so hateful?

NEEL: When Walter's away, my mind starts to vegetate. Don't hold it against me.

SOUHAYLA: People say he's fallen in battle.

NEEL: People say lots of things.

SOUHAYLA: Did he really sleep here last night?

Several bombs in the distance, fairly close together.

NEEL: You love him!

SOUHAYLA: I like him!

NEEL: It's unbelievable!

SOUHAYLA: What's unbelievable?

Several bombs in the distance, fairly close together.

NEEL: Being that jealous! You're jealous, Souhayla.

SOUHAYLA: What am I jealous of?

NEEL: Of Nelly. You're jealous because she's getting married while you, poor Souhayla, you're fat and ugly. No one will ever want you.

SOUHAYLA: You're horrible!

NEEL: Poor Souhayla! You were born in the wrong century! You aren't very pretty and these days people can't be forced to marry just anyone!

SOUHAYLA: Ne…Neel.

NEEL: To have any hope of getting married, you'd have to have been born into one of those rich families in the middle ages where looks ddin't matter; but it's not just that you're not pretty, you…

33

NAZHA: (*Entering and interrupting.*) She'll be as radiant as the sun!

SOUHAYLA: I want you to know, Neel, that what you just said was very hurtful and –

NAZHA: Someone's coming up the stairs!

NEEL: It's my father with the mutton!

NAZHA: What a racket!

NEYIF enters, but he stays in the doorway.

NEYIF: A knife! Quick! A dagger! A big one! A proper murderer's knife. The kind that really slices! A knife, I said! A knife so I can finish it off once and for all! Fucking bastard shit! Nazha! I told you to bring me a big knife!

NAZHA: Come in! Come inside! We'll see about the knife later. Come inside for now!

NEYIF: Stop arguing! It's still alive, I had to leave the butcher's in a hurry…They bombed the shit out of it!

NEYIF is visibly fighting with a sheep that is determined to get into the apartment.

NEYIF: Would you bring me a knife so I can finish him off, so I can Julius Caesar him for you (*The sheep bleats.*). THE BIG KNIFE.

NEEL: You're going to slit its throat?

NEYIF: No, I'm going to cut his toenails! Hurry up and stop arguing!

A sharp whistle. Bombs start falling again very close by.

NEEL: A.D.C. 470 with an incendiary head, those are vicious! Take cover!

Violent explosion.

NEYIF: Stupid sheep! It's biting my ankles!

NAZHA: Well, knock it out!

NEEL: Papa!

NEYIF: What do you want me to knock it out with?

NAZHA: With the hammer! Neel, get the hammer!

NEYIF: Never mind the hammer, just bring me the big knife.

SOUHAYLA: Where is it? I'll get it…

NEYIF: In the second drawer in the kitchen cabinet!

The sheep bleats.

Shut up!

NAZHA: Just knock it out, for fuck's sake. It'll be cleaner that way.

NEEL: You're not going to slit its throat right on the landing!

A violent explosion.

NEYIF: Can you come and take over for a minute!

NEEL: Give me the sheep!

NAZHA: Don't let it get inside! If it shits on the carpet I'll slit *your* throat.

NEEL: You have to be gentle with it!

SOUHAYLA: I couldn't find the knife but you could try these sewing scissors.

NEYIF: They're not very sharp, but they'll do the job.

A violent explosion.

Come on!

NEEL: You're not going to cut the sheep's throat, Papa!

NEYIF: Don't get sentimental! We have to kill it or there won't be any wedding meal! Come here my little lamb chop!

SOUHAYLA: Isn't it getting a bit dangerous to stay up here?

NAZHA: Watch the carpet!

The sheep bleats.

NEEL: You're scaring it!

NAZHA: Give him back the sheep, Neel.

NEYIF: Give me the sheep!

NEEL: No!

A violent explosion.

SOUHAYLA: Come here, Neel darling! You shouldn't see this.

NEYIF: Alright! A man's gotta do what a man's gotta do.

NAZHA: Watch the carpet!

NEEL: Nelly! Nelly!

A violent explosion.

SOUHAYLA: The bombing is getting close again! We have to shut the windows!

NEYIF: Now then! How are you supposed to cut a sheep's throat?

NEEL: Nelly! He's going to slaughter the sheep! Wake up, Nelly! He's going to slit its throat!

NEYIF: Shit! This is disgusting!

Agonised cries from the sheep. A violent explosion.

Fucking shit…

NAZHA: The heart! Aim for the heart!

NEYIF: Ah fuck! Die, you stupid turd, will you shut up and die.

Agonised cries from the sheep.

NAZHA: Watch the carpet!

NEEL: Nelly! Nelly! It's the sheep they're killing for your wedding! Nelly!

NELLY: When are we going to Berdawnay?

Agonised cries from the sheep. Machine gun fire. A violent explosion.

When are we going to Berdawnay?

NEYIF: Die, you bastard! Die!

Agonised cries from the sheep.

SOUHAYLA: Stop singing lullabies to it and just finish it off for fucks sake! Die, you fucker! Die, you bastard! Die!

Machine gun fire.

Do you have anything else to say, hmm?

Agonised cries from the sheep.

Any last words?

The sheep bleats.

What? (*She imitates bleat.*) Behhh? (*A punch.*) Behhh, you little swine? (*A punch.*)
That's the last behhh from you. (*One last hard punch. The sheep dies.*)

NEYIF: The bastard really hung on!

NEEL: That's a surprise in this fucked up country!

NAZHA: Neel, come and help me, we have to shut the windows, it's pouring with rain outside. Come, my dear, don't look at that anymore!

NELLY: (*Off.*) Mama! There are shadows everywhere. Berdawnay has been destroyed! Run Mama! They're going to kill you! Run! Mama!

NAZHA: I'm coming, Nelly. I'm coming.

Machine guns. NAZHA exits. SOUHAYLA goes to help NEEL close the window.

A hurricane-like wind.

SOUHAYLA: Look down there! There's a bus on fire!

NEEL: Full of children!

SOUHAYLA: The soldiers are still shooting! Neel! Don't look at it!

NEEL: Where do you WANT me to look?

SOUHAYLA: I'm telling you, we'd be better off downstairs!

NEYIF: We don't have time to go downstairs. Now that the sheep is dead, we can really get started!

NEEL: We're going to eat a corpse!

NEYIF: At least we're going to eat!

Machine gun fire.

Act Two

NEYIF is skinning the sheep, which is hanging from the ceiling. A pail underneath the sheep catches the dripping blood.

NEYIF: Is Nelly getting ready?

NAZHA: When did she ever stop getting ready? Right now she's drying herself off. She's looking at herself in the mirror. She's crowning her head with flowers.

NEYIF: I'm hungry.

NAZHA: Flowers…red ones and blue ones, fragrant ones, wild rose and sprigs of cherry blossoms, daisies around her wrists. Our daughter will be beautiful.

NEYIF: This bugger doesn't want to let go of his skin. Where's Neel? Why isn't he helping me?!

NAZHA: It sounds like lots of people are coming to the wedding.

NEYIF: I should hope so! Neel! Neel! Shit! What the hell are you doing?

NEEL: (*Off.*) I'm shining my shoes!

NEYIF: Get in here and hold the fucking hooves!

NAZHA: He has to help me set up the table too!

NEYIF: Did you hear me?!

NEEL: (*Off.*) I'm shining my shoes! I'll come when I'm finished shining my shoes!

NAZHA: He's not in the cheeriest of moods! Leave him alone!

NELLY: (*Off.*) Are we going to eat kneffay?

NEEL: (*Off.*) We're gonna eat so much we'll be shitting kneffay for weeks!

NEYIF: Kids! They don't make your life any bloody easier… they do everything they can to poison it!

NEEL: (*Off.*) That's a load of crap!

NEYIF: Shut up, you little worm!

The siren of an ambulance racing down the street.

(*To the ambulance.*) I hope you die!

NAZHA: Maybe they'll be bombing at 4:00! With a little bit of luck, no one will come!

NEYIF: You mean we'd have put ourselves through all this shit for nothing!

NAZHA: Do you remember our wedding?

NEYIF: It was crap! It rained, you had 'cramps'. Three days before we could finally fuck! Now that hurt!

NAZHA: What are you talking about? It was sunny! You remember! We looked gorgeous!

NEYIF: Of course! No kids! People look great when they don't have kids. What do you think turned me into such a miserable bastard? Your scaly skin? It's no different from mine. Your grey hair? It's just a colour like any other. What do you think, huh, my little dumpling? Your plumpness? That, at least, is still exquisite!

NAZHA: I don't want to talk about all that, Neyif! Let's just drop it!

NEYIF: Ah! I know where you're trying to lead me, my dear! But there won't be any tender, tacky reminiscences. We're not going to sit side by side facing the guests and wax lyrical about that special, loving day when we were joined in wedded bliss! Forget it! I'll tell you what repulses me about you, Nazha…

NEEL enters.

NEEL: Here I am! Are we going to skin this fucking sheep?

NEYIF: Get the fuck out of here! I didn't ring for you!

NEEL: Mama!

NEYIF: I said get out, or else I'll take off my belt! Your bad marks at school last year will seem like nothing…get out you piece of camel snot!

NEEL exits.

(*Back to NAZHA.*) I haven't finished! Stand up!

NAZHA: Neyif –

NEYIF: I said stand up! On your feet! Or else I'll hit something…and it's not domestic violence here, it's just part of my nature. On your feet!

NAZHA: Neyif – Neyif –

NEYIF: Stand up!

NAZHA: Calm down! Relax! There we go.

The thunderstorm and bombing wreak havoc.

NEYIF: Do you smell that odour of freshly cut flesh, Nazha? You might think it's coming from the sheep over there! Do you smell it? It's the smell of your crotch, Nazha! Blood! It's that stench that I can't stand anymore!

NAZHA: My God – Neyif!

NEYIF: Shut up! It's that faint smell, Nazha, so bitter, almost like mould! That smell that I saw take shape one day, slowly, layer by layer! Then I saw it get bigger and bigger, until it filled up your greedy little belly that continued to swell and swell…

NAZHA: Neyif! Neyif! I can't take this!

NEYIF: It grew bigger than a cannonball! And then one day, without warning, it burst open! Completely exploded – right up to the stars! There was nothing left then, not of you, or of me! Or of our marriage, and even less of the memory of our wedding! There was nothing left but our newborn daughter, a larva! Soft and formless and infested with that incredibly vile stench! And then, you wanted to give it a name, teach it to walk, you wanted me to go 'coochi-coo' and all that crap, dress it, let it climb on my shoulders, teach it about the world, be a father to it, and today, after thirty years of this daily poisoning, you're determined to make a party for it while bombs are dropping all over the place. Poor Nazha, you must be living in some kind of dream world too! You'll see, the war is going to gobble up your Nelly and us. Today, when people realize there's no fiancé, that there never was a fiancé, maybe they'll have the guts to kill us. Then it'll all be over...

NAZHA: I don't think I feel very well!!

NEYIF: ...and we'll all be better off!

NAZHA staggers.

They'll string us up and that'll be the end of it.

NAZHA goes to the window, opens it wide.

The shells and the thunder have been wreaking havoc in the neighbourhood for a while.

NAZHA: Dear God! Marry my daughter! Marry my daughter! She's still asleep, lovely as a flower of the sea. Find her a husband! A husband who will make her happy, a sincere and gentle husband, who will stay awake all night to watch over her sleep! And make sure they all come – men and women – to celebrate her wedding, and have them wear their most beautiful clothes! Nelly's eyes are still shut but they'll see inside her, they'll see through her, they'll want to inhabit her, they'll look everywhere for extraordinary treasures to throw at her feet and the sweetest perfumes to anoint my sleepwalker on her journey!

NELLY: (*Off.*) Mama! Why are you running away? Stay! I remember the countryside, how you ran towards me among the cedars! The sky was so blue! And your arms around my heart! Why did you die, Mama? Why did you leave? Don't run so fast! Don't run away! Stay! Stay!

NAZHA: Where will she find the safety to talk like this? Where will she find the salvation that brings peace and rest? Salvation My Lord! That same salvation that, in your grace, you showed me at the very moment of her birth. Do you remember: You appeared to me in all your whiteness, an extravagant presence. Then I felt, I felt this incredibly sweet movement! Something inside me was stretching out, carrying me away. They said to me 'push, push,' but I was looking at the universe! The universe between my legs, it slid out of me, it escaped. Do you remember that deliverance, my Lord? What came out of my belly had no body – it was a light I felt slip out of me, a light that has illuminated my whole life! Dear God, that light that spilled out of my depths was your own! Where are you? Where is your grace? Your salvation? Ahh! There is no salvation possible in this carnage! All there is is dust, dust, and more dust!

Machine gun fire.

NEYIF: Nazha! The snipers are shooting at us!

NAZHA: I don't give a shit.

Nearby explosion. A storm erupts outside the windows. The electricity goes off.

(*Still at the window.*) I don't care! Do you hear me, you bunch of animals! I don't care! (*An explosion.*). You can shove your grenades up each others' arses for all I care!

An incredibly violent explosion. The shutters fly open, the windows also.

The rain and the wind burst in.

You douchebags!

SOUHAYLA enters.

SOUHAYLA: I'm in a total panic! I'm going to pieces!

An explosion.

NAZHA: You Neanderthals!

NEEL enters.

NEEL: Mama, Mama, Nelly's crying. She's asleep and she's crying!

Machine gun fire.

NAZHA: You slimebuckets!

NEYIF: Go back and stay with your sister. I'm trying to calm your mother down.

SOUHAYLA: I'll come with you.

NEEL and SOUHAYLA exit. NAZHA grabs a dish and makes to throw it out the window.

NAZHA: We'll throw kibbeh at our brave soldiers! You'll see! We'll make them slosh around in hummus!

NEYIF: No! Not the hummus…

An explosion.

Nazha, not the hummus, no, I'm begging you…

NAZHA throws the dish out the window. Machine gun fire.

NAZHA: Troglodytes!

NEYIF: She's out of control!

Machine gun fire.

NAZHA: Fascists!

NEYIF: Nazha! Calm down!

NAZHA: I'm calming down. I am calm. I'm very calm!

SOUHAYLA and NEEL enter.

SOUHAYLA: Nazha, Nazha, Nelly is all (*She gestures.*) hunched up – hun – hundled –

NEEL: Huddled up!

SOUHAYLA: That's it! Under the bathroom sink! Could she be dead?!

NAZHA: That's her spot! Don't wake her up! It could be awful!

NEYIF: Calm down! Calm down, I said, everybody calm down! (*Silence.*) Alright. The guests will start arriving soon, so let's have some calm.

NAZHA: The wedding, the wedding! What a wedding we'll have!

SOUHAYLA: You're right! Fucking right. Nothing else matters except the wedding! Neel! Neel come on, we're going to set up the table!

NAZHA: Turn the lights on! It's really dark in here.

NEEL: There's no electricity!

SOUHAYLA: I forgot to bring up the warra arrishe and the baba ghanouj. I'll go and get them.

SOUHAYLA exits.

NEYIF: What are we going to do about her?

NAZHA: We could tell her! She won't hold it against us! She's so nice, so dim!

NEEL: You want to tell her that Nelly isn't getting married after all – that we've told everyone the fiancé is arriving at 4:00, but the whole thing has just been a big joke? For God's sake! She'll die of pleasure! It'll make her so happy she might get pregnant, just like that, without warning!

NEYIF: Maybe she suspects! Let's pull out now before we really get in over our heads!

NEEL: No, no. She's a lot sneakier than we think. If she had the slightest suspicion, why would she have slaved away with her hummus and her fassoulia and her baba ghanouj?!

NAZHA: And her beyleywa!

NEEL: And her beyleywa! Holy shit! We all know how much beyleywa costs! No! No! If she had any doubts about the fiancé, she wouldn't have worked so hard; you'd think she was preparing for her own wedding!

NEYIF: None of this is getting us anywhere! If we tell her, what's the worst that can happen?

NAZHA: All the women in the neighbourhood will find out!

NEEL: And then none of them will come?

NAZHA: None of them will come!

NEYIF: Let's tell her then! In one fell swoop we'll get rid of all the scum around here.

NAZHA: How are we going to explain to all the nosey neighbours why we've cancelled the wedding?

NEEL: We'll say the fiancé couldn't come because of the situation, and we'll postpone the whole thing until a later date!

NAZHA: It will break Nelly's heart!

NEYIF: She's so convinced! How will she feel tonight, at 7:00, and at 8:00? Will she still be waiting for her fiancé? Poor Nelly! Eventually, she'll realise! Then maybe she'll throw herself out of the window! It's a terrible thing when a fiancé doesn't show up! Especially if he doesn't exist!

NELLY: (*Off.*) My fiancé will come!

NAZHA: We can't back out!

NEYIF: Fine! So we won't back out!

NEEL: Fuck it!

NAZHA: Nelly, darling, wouldn't you like to come and sit with us for a few minutes?

NELLY: (*Off.*) Today, I'll sit at your side dressed in white.

NAZHA: As you wish, darling!

NEYIF: What else can we do but go ahead with it!

NEEL: Fuck it!

NELLY: (*Off.*) Mama.

NAZHA: Yes, Nelly?

NELLY: (*Off.*) Why is the war so beautiful? Why can't I take my eyes off it? These fireworks! It's so breathtaking Mama, I'm kneeling, wide awake, at the open window, savouring the destruction! It's all so beautiful. Down below buildings are crumbling; the city falling to its knees, there are fires dancing in the middle of the storm, a tree is exploding!

NAZHA: Nelly! Shut the window and keep getting dressed, darling. Don't look!

NELLY: (*Off.*) Mama!

NAZHA: Yes, Nelly?

NELLY: (*Off.*) Are the great artists of this country preparing a big celebration? Who else could create something so spellbinding as war. Yesterday, yes, I think it was yesterday, I woke up in the middle of the night, and I looked out the window and I saw flames coming from our neighbour's apartment! I saw our neighbour jump off her balcony, holding her baby in her arms. As she fell, she dropped him, screamed something and then smashed into the pavement. Her child exploded in mid-air, skewered by a bolt of lightning that came out of the night. Mama, how can something so hideous be so beautiful? Mama, how can something so beautiful?... Mama, how can...

SOUHAYLA enters.

SOUHAYLA: I brought some candles! People will think we turned the lights off on purpose – for ambience!

NAZHA: Just like in Europe – by candlelight!

NEYIF: Why don't you give me a hand so we can set up this bitch of a table.

SOUHAYLA: There we go! What else is there left to do!

NAZHA: The battenjen and the coussa to stuff!

SOUHAYLA: Well, let's get stuffing!

NAZHA: I hope the electricity comes back on for the mutton!

NEYIF: Well, I, for one, am starting to get very hungry.

NEEL: Shit, this table is heavy!

NAZHA: Raw mutton! That would be a real faux-pas!

SOUHAYLA: In wartime people shouldn't complain!

NAZHA: But, you know, some people will complain no matter what!

SOUHAYLA: Now that's true. The Armenian says our war isn't so bad. He says lots of countries have been through a lot worse than we have. According to him some people – the Armenians, for example – have lived through far worse atrocities. He says compared to the Armenians, we're just a bunch of lightweights.

NAZHA: What does that bastard know about our history?! About our country?! What the fuck does that piece of smegma know about it?! That lice-infested baboon's ass! He disgusts me! He makes me seethe, that shrivelled foreskin of an Armenian! Fuck it! He drives me over the hedge!

NEEL: Edge!

NAZHA: Now what?! I'm warning you, you little twat, I won't put up with your mental defectiveness much longer! If your brain doesn't stop its high-flying acrobatics, I'll break its fucking trapeze!

NEEL: But I didn't do anything!

NEYIF: Alright! Calm down!

NEEL: All I did was say edge! I said edge because you said hedge!

NAZHA: What do you mean I said hedge? When did I say hedge?

SOUHAYLA: Never mind, it's nothing… She said what you're supposed to say! That's all.

NEYIF: That's right, that's all!

NEEL: She said hedge…

NEYIF: Neel! That's enough!

NEEL: I'm sick and tired of this! The minute I open my mouth everyone shouts at me! If I'd said *hedge*, you'd all have shouted at me it's *edge*!

SOUHAYLA: What's all this about hedge and edge?

NAZHA: Let's not talk about it anymore! I'd rather talk about that cockroach of an Armenian! Thank God they're not all like him!

NEYIF: Come on son! Keep screwing those legs in! I'm going to get the plates.

NEYIF exits.

NEEL: 'He drives me over the hedge!' Over the edge, not over the hedge!

SOUHAYLA: So, anyway, according to him it was the Armenians who suffered the worst massacre in history! He even claims it's etched into his flesh! He said it was the worst massacre ever!

NEEL: 'Over the hedge!' That's the best one yet!

NAZHA: He doesn't know a thing! What about five hundred years ago when the Mamelukes massacred the whole area, what was that supposed to be? A manicure?

SOUHAYLA: Exactly!

NEEL: I've got to tell my friends that one. It's hilarious! 'Over the hedge!' 'Over the hedge!'

The electricity comes back on. All cheer.

ALL: Ahhh!!

NAZHA: Hurry up Neyif! We have to put the sheep in the oven! Quick! Before the power goes off again!

NEYIF: (*Off.*) Coming!

NAZHA: Good! Now, cut me off that piece there! And then that one! Don't turn the oven up too high, and make sure you baste it well with the arak, alright?

NEYIF: Shit! All this is making me hungry!

The electricity goes off. All groan.

ALL: Ohh!!

NAZHA: Oh no! It's awful! It's so awful! Everything's going wrong today!

NEEL: We're going to eat the mutton cold – and raw! Don't say I didn't warn you!

NEYIF: We'll just leave the whole thing in the oven. When the electricity comes back on, it'll be all ready!

NAZHA: I'll come and help you! You won't know how to do it!

NAZHA and NEYIF exit.

NEEL: We're going to eat the mutton raw! With our hands! We'll fight over the best pieces! We'll club each other with the kidneys!

SOUHAYLA: You're disgraceful! So rude and vulgar! Neel, I'm really disappointed in you! You used to be so sweet…

NEEL: Oh no! Leave the fucking sentimentality to other people! There's no room for that kind of shit round here. Everyone uses it to trick me. No one here knows how to talk in dynamite! Not one single person. Except for Walter! He's amazing! He blasts through everything! He leaves everything sparkling! Spic and span! You know what he says to people who get too close to him?

SOUHAYLA: What does he say?

NEEL: He raises his arm and shouts: 'I'm Walter! A walking neutron bomb. I've come to recite to you a poem that will help you rest in peace!' And he raises his gun and empties his three clips. Tatatatatatatatatatata-tatatata and tatatatatatatata and tatatatatatatatatatata. I've seen him do it.

SOUHAYLA: He used to come downstairs to my place and sit with me and guess what he would do?

NEEL: He would rip off his clothes and run after you shouting, 'I'm gonna rape you, Souhayla, I'm gonna rape you!'

SOUHAYLA: He used to come and read me his poems. Poems he'd written himself. Your brother could have been a great poet!

NEEL: He still can be! Tatatatatatatatatatatatatatatata! That's the title of his latest poem.

SOUHAYLA: Is he coming to the wedding?

NEEL: What wedding?

SOUHAYLA: There's only one for two hundred miles around. There aren't any others, you little brat! Only one that everyone's talking about!

NEEL: Everyone?

SOUHAYLA: Everyone! Everyone's talking about it because everyone's wondering about Nelly's famous fiancé! They're wondering – and I'm wondering too – how your sister managed to snare such a rich and handsome European!

NEEL: My sister's gorgeous!

SOUHAYLA: She's attractive, but she's always asleep.

NEEL: So?

SOUHAYLA: So?

NEEL: So?

SOUHAYLA: So, I really don't understand how Nelly could have met such a fiancé when so many normal girls, I mean, normal in their heads, can still only hope.

NEEL: Don't get so excited. Because there isn't going to be a wedding! This is all a great big practical joke. There won't be any wedding because there isn't any fiancé!

SOUHAYLA: You're – euh – euh – disgusting! Yes! That's it! Disgusting! The men in the neighbourhood used to say a lot of nasty things about Walter! But now I see the truth! You're the snake!

NEEL: I never whistled at women.

SOUHAYLA: Neither did Walter.

NEEL: Yes he did.

SOUHAYLA: You're lying through your teeth! Walter was far too intelligent to sink so low. He was generous, his face was like a clear blue sky...and I loved him... I loved him... But he didn't love me! And now he's dead. It's such a tragedy! I can't take it any more, I'm cracking up, yes, that's it! I'm having a breakdown! I admit it! (*She sobs.*)

NEEL: Souhayla! I'm trying to cheer you up by telling you that Nelly won't be getting married since there's NO HUSBAND. But you don't believe me! You really are stupid!

SOUHAYLA: Well! I didn't come up here to talk to you, or to be insulted. You can say I'll be back later. And count yourself lucky that I'm not telling your mother, you little fool!

NEEL: Tickle my tool!

SOUHAYLA exits.

Bombing in the distance. A bomb explodes with distinction.

A shining coral! Quick! A wish! They do unbelievable damage, but they have these incredible names! A shining coral! Some people die in style! Nelly!...

NELLY: (*Off.*) Softly, Neel! I'm right here!

NEEL: Come out!

NELLY: (*Off.*) It's nicer to stay in the darkness! Your voice is running around. Now I can see it hiding under the armchair. Like when you were little, do you remember?

NEEL: Little! I used to be little?

NELLY: (*Off.*) When Mama did the housework, she would stack up all the living room furniture and drape the carpet over the pile! It would make a tent and you would crawl inside! You would stay hiding in there! And I used to call you: Neel! Come and see me, I'm all alone! There's no one in my dreams! Come on my little brother, where are you?

NEEL: I don't remember!

NELLY: (*Off.*) And then I would hide under the sofa – then you'd start looking for me and you would call me: 'Nelly, where are you? Look outside, there's a building on fire, quick, we have to escape, pack our suitcases and go like Aunt Bosra who left with her five daughters!!' And then I would come out of hiding and you would run to me, jump into my arms, kiss me, you loved me so much!

NEEL: You're telling me another one of your 'endless' stories!

NELLY: (*Off.*) The end is coming! We just have to prepare the wedding, Neel. Have faith. Walter will be here soon. We'll play together, just like he promised you. Between the three of us, the war won't stand a chance. I'm getting married, Neel, I'm getting married.

NEEL: You really do need a fiancé for a wedding!

NELLY: (*Off.*) Don't you believe in anything anymore? What about fairies, and pumpkins and ice cream and sugar plums?

NEEL: Nelly! My dear sweet sister! Here, people only talk about war!

NELLY: (*Off.*) Do you remember the last poem Walter wrote?

NEEL: Tatatatatatatatatatatatatatata.

NELLY: It was a poem about birds, love and light.

NEEL: Walter has disappeared, Nelly. Disappeared. He might even be dead and all the poetry in the world is dead with him.

NELLY: (*Off.*) You shouldn't talk about death, Neel.

NEEL: But I shouldn't be where I am! Period! I'm caught in a story too complicated for my age! The moment I was born they took me away and they tied me up, and ever since then they've been forcing me to watch a bad film! With a terrible plot! A bad film in which from beginning to end people get fucked up the arse by one prick after another. So you understand, Nelly, I can't smile at your fairy tales. I just see arses and cocks! Endless slurping of arseholes! Big fat cocks rammed up to the hilt in juicy vaginas! Dykes, poofs, dogs with enormous drooling and foaming dicks! Green tongues lapping up the foam that's frothing and overflowing! Do you want some, here you go. Blow job after blow job, a whirl of shafts and knobs, vomiting, ravenous cunts and cadaverous penises, all spinning around, people sucking each other off all over the place, coming and going here and there, and all you can hear are obscene moans and there's a guy walking around with his prick hanging below his knees, and he stabs another guy and makes him swallow big mouthfuls of his shit, and it goes on and on, over and over, and he pisses on him, and the other asks for more but the first guy is empty so he slits open the other guy's thing, and he sprays himself with the blood that spurts out, and he sticks his hand in through the navel to scrape the bottom of the guy's stomach, then he grabs the guy's intestines and his liver and he pulls on them, Nelly, he tugs on them, he pulls on them again, and then he shoots the guy, he blasts him, waving his cause like a banner, he shoots him, do you understand? He shoots him, a man, he shoots him and a man falls because he's empty, one less Nelly, one less man, surely the son of a mother! What…what…What will she do now without him?

Who will go to get the lettuce that smells like fish at the fucking Armenian's! Who? Who? He's dead! He's dead! He's dead!

NELLY: (*Off.*) Don't fall little brother! Today is my wedding day! Have faith! Listen outside, it's the war digging its own grave with a great blasting of shells! The day is near, believe me, the day when our tired faces will once again be flooded with light.

Act Three

The table is set up. It is beautiful. Large. White. Plates. Cutlery. Candles. The storm is increasingly ferocious. But is it really the storm? NAZHA is in a slip and high heels. NEEL is in his underwear and NEYIF is in his undershirt and very fancy trousers. They are getting dressed. They are getting ready.

NEYIF: We don't have much time left!

NEEL: You're telling me – it's gone three!

NEYIF: It smells good! Shit, I'm hungry!

NEEL: We're going to eat the mutton raw!

NEYIF: We might be lucky, the electricity could come back on!

NEEL: It'll go off again straight away!

NEYIF: Go and get dressed instead of arguing!

NEEL: I already told you it'll start the same way. It always starts the same way, always always always…

NEYIF: Get dressed!!

NEEL: I'd love to but I can't find my wedding trousers. My dress trousers for special occasions!

NEYIF: I don't care! I'm tired of seeing you naked!

NEEL: Mama! I can't find my dress trousers!

NEYIF: Let your mother get dressed! All she was wearing a little while ago was her black slip!

NAZHA: (*Off.*) Hey!

She enters.

I'm still only wearing my black slip!

NEYIF: That doesn't surprise me! You get dressed at a snail's pace!

NAZHA: That may be! But at least I'm attractive when I dress up! I don't have a pot belly! I don't stink of cigar smoke, and I don't have little grey hairs sticking out of my dress! I smell nice! You aesthetic disaster!

NEEL: Alright, I'm getting out of here. Go ahead, it's time for your little duet!

NEEL exits.

NEYIF: So, go on. I'm waiting.

NAZHA: I'm not getting sucked into your little game! I'm not bursting with hatred! But you, poor Neyif, you're another story. Poor Neyif. I pity you! You're skinny! And ugly! What has your life been apart from me?

NEYIF: Stop! You're making me cry!

NAZHA: Ha! Too late my dear, that's your problem! Cry! You aren't capable of crying! All you can do is get angry!

NEYIF: Shut up! You're starting to get on my nerves!

NAZHA: That's what's going to kill you! There's so much anger coursing through your veins that one day your heart's going to confuse your anger with your blood, and instead of pumping the one, it'll pump the other! Then I'll finally see you blow up for good!

NEYIF: That'll make your day, won't it!

NAZHA: Too right. I'll laugh my head off and spit on your corpse.

NEYIF: Who gives a shit, I'll be dead, I won't feel a thing!

NAZHA: That's just it, you've never felt anything! You don't cry anymore, you never get a hard on, you hardly even fart anymore! You're cold and unfeeling!

NEYIF: There we go. Now we're getting somewhere. That's what I was waiting for. Feelings! Feelings!

NAZHA: Yes, feelings! Feelings!

NEYIF: You sound like an aging actress! Feeelings, nothing more than feeelings, how many tons of feelings do you think there are outside? You can hear their fucking feelings falling on our heads! A well-aimed D.C.4, what do you think that is? How am I supposed to love, to get a hard on, fart and shit, that's right, SHIT, when all over the place people are venting their feeeelings! Well, I don't have any feelings. I don't want to have any, either, and I don't give a fuck about your feelings, Nazha, about their feelings, about anybody's feelings! If those guys out there weren't so busy dealing with their feeeelings and their own little selves maybe we wouldn't be in this mess!

NAZHA: You're crying?

NEYIF: Yes, I'm crying!

NAZHA: Neyif, my love! Anything is possible!

A terrible explosion followed by a clap of thunder, followed by several whistles, other explosions, other claps of thunder. NEEL enters, still in his underwear.

NEEL: I give up! Where are my dress trousers?

NAZHA: They're outside! On the clothesline!

NEEL: Oh great! That's just great! What the fuck am I going to do without my dress trousers! It's been pissing down and there are snipers everywhere! How am I going to get my them now?

NEYIF: You're a pain in the arse, Neel! You're annoying your poor mother and me! Is that getting through to you? The two of us are stirring up the past and you prance back in here bleating on about your trousers! I don't give a flying fuck about your trousers, I want to talk to your mother, do you hear me? So just piss off or I'm going to lose my temper!

NEEL: It's not fair!

NEEL exits.

NAZHA: Kiss me!

NEYIF: Nazha!

NAZHA: Kiss me, I said!

They kiss. Bombs are still falling in the distance, and increasingly closer. The storm continues.

NEYIF: Let's make love!

NAZHA: On the table!

NEYIF: On the table!!

NAZHA: In the keshk!

NEYIF: I'm gonna do to you what you do to the coussa.

NAZHA: Yes, yes. Fill me up. Stuff your little battenjen.

NEYIF: I'm getting a hard on, holy fuck. I'm getting a hard on.

NAZHA: My darling! Don't worry, I can't have children anymore!

NEYIF: Lift up your slip.

NAZHA: Give me your tongue!

NEYIF: I'd forgotten what your arse feels like!

NAZHA: I love you! I love you! You're still so handsome!

NEYIF: In wartime, life begins at fifty!

NAZHA takes off her skirt. The electricity comes back on.

NAZHA: Aah! The electricity is back on! Quick! The mutton!

NEYIF: Nazha! Who gives a fuck about the mutton! We'd just turned into lions again. Where are you going?

NAZHA: The mutton!

She exits.

NEYIF: I've had it! If that's the way it's going to be! It's either me or the mutton! Neel! You want your dress trousers, you little toe-rag? *I'll* go and get them.

NEYIF leaves the apartment.

NELLY: (*Off.*) When are we going to Berdawnay?

NEEL: Next Friday…(*Shouting down the stairs after NEYIF.*) Papa! Come back! Come back! Forget about the trousers, I'll wear any old pair! It's no problem!

NELLY: (*Off.*) Next Friday?

NEEL: Next Friday! Mama, Mama, Papa will get himself killed! He's outside and he's shouting!

NAZHA enters and joins NEEL on the balcony.

NAZHA: Neyif! Wait! I'll come with you! Wait for me! Don't die without me, I want to get out of here, too!

NEEL: Mama, stay here!

NAZHA struggles with NEEL.

NAZHA: Let go of me! Let go of me! I want to run into the arms of my love!

NAZHA exits.

NEEL: She can be so stupid sometimes! Mama! Stay here! Walter! Fuck it Walter, I really need you here!

NEEL goes back onto the balcony.

NELLY: (*Off.*) Next Friday?… Next Friday in Berdawnay…to eat kneffay… There's no one left! There's only me! I'm always so sleepy! Naked in the middle of the war! What do they all have to shout about? They must think my fiancé isn't going to come, so they've left. (*Shouting.*) Hey, my fiancé is going to come! They don't hear me, they think I'm still asleep. Maybe I actually am asleep this very moment. 'But you're here, Nelly! With your eyes open.' I don't know anymore. 'You don't know anymore if you're dreaming or not?' No, Nelly, I don't know anymore. Before, in my dreams, I'd sometimes turn into a big tree; I'd catch fire in the middle of a wood, I'd run with all my roots and throw myself over a cliff. Then I would wake

up. 'You would wake up?' Yes, I would wake up and I
would know what the words 'waking up' meant: finding
a peaceful blue sky, a world very different from the one
in my dreams, and then yes, I would know that I'd been
dreaming and that I had just woken up. 'And now?' Now?
'No, no, don't cry, Nelly.' I can't! Now all I dream about
is the toilet, the door and the concrete wall. And when I
wake up, I see the same door, Nelly, the same concrete
wall, and that's it. Now I no longer know where I am Nelly.
Can you help me? 'I can't do anything, Nelly. Nothing.'

NEEL: (*Off.*) He did it! He did it! He got my trousers!

NAZHA: (*Off.*) It's a miracle! A real miracle!

NEYIF arrives flanked by NAZHA and NEEL. Wet. Trembling.

NEEL: Is my father cool or what!

NEYIF: They shot at me!

NEEL: Did you think they'd toss petunias at you!

NAZHA: Sit down!

NEYIF: Shit!

NELLY: (*Off.*) Mama!

NAZHA: I'm coming, Nelly, I'm coming!

NAZHA exits

MAN'S VOICE: Hey, Neyif!

NEEL: I think someone's calling you!

VOICE: Neyif!

NEYIF goes to the balcony.

NEYIF: Hello Lteff

VOICE: I've brought the dress!

NEYIF: Come on up!

VOICE: No! No! They're going to start bombing again! Here,
catch!

The man in the street throws him a package.

NEYIF: Take this to your sister!

NEEL: The dress maker didn't get blown up?

NEEL exits.

NEYIF: This fucking life! Fucking shit! What a life. It's just a bag of donkey farts. Ahh! Why don't they just put a bullet through my head and get it over with! Shit! I'm hungry!

NEEL enters.

NEEL: Thanks for my trousers, Papa! …but you know, that was a stupid thing to do! Papa. Papa.

NEYIF: Neel! Calm down! OK? There is a lot of electricity in the air!

NEEL: There's not even enough to cook the mutton! Electricity in the air! You must be joking!

NEYIF: No, it's a figure of speech!

NEEL: Yeah! A figure of speech! And when someone says to you 'You drive me over the hedge', would you call that a figure of speech, too?

NEYIF: Neel! Please, let's talk calmly, do you mind? Without raising your voice, alright?

NEEL grunts.

We're going to have a good time, Neel, aren't we? They're all going to come and they're going to die of jealousy when they see our wedding table! Their tongues will be hanging out!

NEEL: Yeah! The guys are going to have their balls in a knot when they see Nelly in her beautiful dress!

NEYIF: We're going to make up incredible stories, you'll see, we'll talk about the fiancé's car!

NEEL: And his villa! And about his servants and the old man who's been his servant since he was small. The servant's name is Darwish!

NEYIF: No! We need something less suspicious-sounding…like Alistair.

NEEL: Yes, it's Alistair who's waiting for Nelly and her fiancé in their villa! We'll tell them the fiancé takes care of an orphanage

NEYIF: We have to find him a name!

NEEL: Yeah! Let's find him a name! Ramón!

NEYIF: Too exotic!… David!

NEEL: No! He's not a David!

NEYIF: Burt, like our plumber!

NEEL: I don't see him as a plumber!

NEYIF: Fine!

NEEL: How about Giancarlo, like Giancarlo Giannini! That'll make him sound more European. Giancarlo!

NEYIF: Giancarlo?

NEEL: Yes! Giancarlo! Not bad, eh?

NEYIF: Giancarlo! I don't know! We'll ask your mother… Nazha! What do you think of Giancarlo?

NAZHA: (*Off.*) I don't know any Giancarlo!

NEEL: Yes you do, Mama… Giancarlo, Nelly's fiancé!

NAZHA: (*Off.*) Oh! You mean François! Oh well, he's a very nice boy!

NEYIF: Well son! She's already come up with a name!

NEEL: François! He sounds like a shoe salesman.

NEYIF: What have you got against shoe salesmen?

NEEL: Nothing, but they usually don't get what they want in life!

NEYIF: What do you know about life?

NEEL: You're right, I don't know much about it!

NEYIF: Lucky bastard! I'd trade places with you anytime.

NEEL: Is that why you spend your life shouting at me?

NEYIF: I don't shout at you, I educate you.

NEEL: Don't worry about educating me. The war is doing a good enough job of it, I swear.

NEYIF: That's enough. Go get dressed.

NEEL: Thanks for getting my trousers, Papa!

NEYIF: It was just a stupid pair of trousers!

NEEL: It's not the trousers, I don't care about the trousers, it's because for a brief moment you turned back into my childhood hero!

NEYIF: Oh, shut up. Go and get dressed!

NEEL: Papa!…

NEYIF: I said go and get dressed! Do you know what time it is? Put your clothes on, so at least two of us will be decent when the guests arrive.

NEEL: And it's started all over again! I knew it, right from the start, I even said so: it always starts the same way, the same way, always always always…

NEEL exits.

NEYIF: Nazha! I'm starving!

A bomb explodes nearby. Another follows.

Nazha! What are you doing?

NEEL: (*Off.*) Oh great! Now I can't find my shoes!

One bomb, and then another. Incredibly violent thunder. The shutters hold.

NAZHA: (*Off, continues singing under NEYIF's lines.*)
It's my dear little Nelly
Our smiling sleeping beauty
Today's the day of awakening
Today's the day that her heart will sing

NEYIF: Nazha? Maybe we should go downstairs until it calms down.

A bomb explodes. The storm. The electricity goes off. NEYIF wants to go see but is pinned to the ground by an explosion.

Neel! Nazha! We have to go downstairs.

An explosion throws NEYIF to the floor.

NEEL: (*Off.*) Where have I put my shoes again! Mama, I can't find my shoes!

Explosions, the walls shake. The windows break, a submachine gun battle takes place very close to the house.

NEYIF: They're shooting at me! That's it, I'm going to die! It's now! I can feel it!

NAZHA: (*Off, continues singing under NEYIF's lines.*)
It's our sweet pretty Nelly
Arising from her bedclothes
To go join hands with her betrothed
Today she'll leave her parent's home.

NEYIF: I don't want to die all alone! Neel! Nazha! Good God, where are you! (*He gets up, another explosion pins him to the ground right away.*)

NEEL: (*Off.*) Shit! Where are my fucking shoes!

NEYIF: They're shooting at me, don't leave me all alone! Nazha! Neel!

NAZHA: (*Off, singing.*) The most beautiful birds in sight

All dance and spin and play

NEYIF: I don't want to die! I don't want to die!

An even worse explosion forces NEYIF to remain on the ground.

NAZHA: (*Off.*) On a carpet of rose petals pink and bright
For Nelly the bride on her wedding day.

Explosions. Sharp whistles. More of them. Explosions. Smoke. Thunder. Rain.

The windows break. The shutters open under the impact. The wedding table doesn't move an inch, still there, still beautiful.

NEYIF: Help! Neel! Nazha!

Explosions. NELLY appears. In her white dress. Smiling. She is stunning. Her words are lucid.

She has extraordinary dignity and grace. She is beautiful, like women who are free.

NELLY: This is it! I'm marching forward! They won't turn ME into a terrified, shrinking mouse! Look at me, I'm walking across the killing fields!

NEYIF: We're going to get blown to bits!

NELLY: I'm looking upwards!

NEYIF: The bombs!

NELLY: I refuse to bow down to the missiles! No! No! The missiles will simply go off course when they see the light streaming from my face!

NEYIF: I don't want to die…

NELLY: Corpses will always rot!

NEEL: Yayyy! I found my shoes!

NELLY: And daisies will always grow back on the battlefields!

Act Four

The sound and lighting are very important to the sense of this act.

The whole family is dressed. Everyone is seated around NELLY. The storm is raging outside.

The electricity comes and goes, wavering, flickering, with the surge and ebb of the storm.

The table is there. Appetising. It is four pm. The clock, if there were one, would chime as much as it wanted. Everyone is waiting. A distant thunderclap. A gust of rain. It is very important for us to feel that all the elements are affecting each other: the winds whip the rain, and the electricity is in turn affected by the rain and wind. A long pause.

NELLY: My fiancé will come.

NEYIF: Er…

> *Long pause.*

NEEL: Walter's the one who won't come.

NAZHA: He'll be here soon.

NEEL: He'll be here soon, he'll be here soon. It's 4:00. He promised me he'd come and play with me before the guests arrive.

> *Long pause. Thunderclap.*

NEYIF: What lousy weather.

NEEL: You can say that again.

> *Long pause.*

NEYIF: Shit. I'm hungry.

> *Pause. He sings to the tune of 'I will survive' – ba ba ba etc. Occasionally singing a few words. This goes on about fourty-five seconds, becoming louder as he gets carried away.*

NAZHA: Stop it!

NEYIF: What do you mean, stop?

NAZHA: I mean you're getting on our nerves. Every time you're hungry you turn into a human juke-box.

NEYIF: I don't care. I'm the head of the household and if I want to sing, I'll sing. (*He sings off and on over the next two pages.*)

A very loud thunderclap.

NEEL: I think God is pissed off with the head of the household.

Very long pause. During which NELLY falls asleep at the table, then wakes up. Then NELLY falls asleep on NEYIF's shoulder. NEEL adjusts his bow-tie. Very long pause. A bomb explodes.

Hmmn, a K72

Pause.

NEYIF: Maybe we can start eating.

NAZHA: We'll wait for the guests.

NEYIF: The guests, the guests.

NEEL: Very funny.

A long pause. A bomb explodes.

A 448 with a rotating head.

NELLY wakes up. Pause.

NEYIF: Let's eat, for fuck's sake. Let's eat.

NAZHA: No.

NEYIF: But no one's going to show up!

NEEL: Of course no one's going to show up! This is all just an illusion. Even the table! Look at it! There's nothing but appetizers! Where is the main dish? Where's the mutton you slaughtered with your own hands, Papa? In the oven? I don't think so! When the guests come, when we tell them the fiancé doesn't exist and that they have to eat the mutton raw, you'll see, they'll hang us up by our feet!

NELLY: My fiancé will come.

NAZHA: Yes, darling, he'll come.

Very long pause.

NEYIF: I'm hungry.

NAZHA: Think about something else.

NEYIF: I can't, I'm hungry.

Two bombs explode. A thunderclap. NELLY falls asleep. Very long pause.

NELLY: When are we going to Berdawnay?

NEEL: Next Friday.

NELLY: Next Friday?

NEEL: Yes.

NELLY: To eat kneffay?

NEEL: Yes.

NELLY: When are we going to Berdawnay?

NEEL: Next Friday.

NELLY: Next Friday?

NEYIF: No, I must be dreaming. I'm dreaming! Tell me this is a dream.

Very long pause.

NELLY: (*Singing.*) The odours spill from the garbage cans
Into the Arab's coffee cups
All they have left is the sky
To dream their dreams
Of lands far away
Because…

NAZHA: She's having a nice dream! Look how she's smiling like the sun!

NEEL: She's singing one of Walter's poems.

NAZHA: Look at her!

NELLY: (*Singing.*) A curse on those who forget
    The beauty of the Mediterranean
    The biggest sea
    In all the world!

Regular bombing begins, every five seconds we hear a whistle followed by a rather violent explosion. The whole neighbourhood is starting to be bombed. During this, NELLY continues to sing.

I pour out the belongings of my heart
Into the Mediterranean
She carries them down
To her deepest waters
There, among the fish and the reefs
My secrets sleep
In her peaceful embrace.

Distant thunder and light bombing. NEYIF starts up his song ('I will survive') again, quietly.

Everyone except NELLY gradually starts to join in. In the middle of NEYIF's song, there is a knock on the door. Everyone stops singing. NEYIF stops. Everyone looks at each other.

NEEL: Fuck! The guests!

SOUHAYLA enters, dressed for the party.

ALL: Souhayla!

SOUHAYLA: Is the fiancé here yet?

NEEL: No.

NAZHA: No.

NEYIF: No.

SOUHAYLA: And the guests?

NEYIF: Not yet.

NAZHA: Not yet.

NEEL: Not yet.

The family starts singing again. SOUHAYLA slowly joins in. NELLY wakes up. She stands.

NELLY: Mama!

All stop singing except SOUHAYLA.

NAZHA: She's woken up!

NELLY: Mama, Mama, it's now!

NAZHA: What, darling?

NELLY: It's now, it's now, he's coming!

SOUHAYLA: Walter?

A huge bomb. Machine gun fire. Another bomb. A very sharp whistle.

NEEL: A 579 BTX! Everyone take cover!

The bombing starts up again. Explosions. NELLY is still standing.

Stay down!

Explosions.

NAZHA: Nelly! Lie down! Lie down!

Ferocious, rhythmic bombing has started. NEEL names all the bombs.

Nelly! Get away from the window!

NEEL: Doshka
Doshka
Doshka
Doshka

NAZHA: Nelly! Get away from the window!

NEEL: Doshka
Doshka

45 BTA 4

The thud of a scud.

SOUHAYLA: Dear God protect us!

NEYIF: I think now we really have to go downstairs.

A bomb falls in front of the house.

SOUHAYLA: (*Shouting.*) Ahhhh! Ahiiii! Yahaaa!

NAZHA: Souhayla!

An explosion which throws everyone violently to the ground.

NELLY sways with the impact.

NEYIF: I'll get the bag of food and we'll go down.

He exits. A bomb explodes in front of the house.

NEEL: D.C.A.
Doshka
Doshka
M16
Kalashnikov
M16
Kalashnikov
Doshka

NAZHA: We have to shut the window. Nelly, lie down! Lie down!

NEEL: Stay down, Mama.
Doshka
Doshka
A black mass
A black pudding

SOUHAYLA: (*Yelling.*) AAAAAYI! I want to get out of here!

NEEL: A black widow alla putanesca!

SOUHAYLA: Stop! Stop for heaven's sake!

NEEL: A Louis XIV

SOUHAYLA: AHHHHHH! AHIIII!

NEEL: A Pius XXII

A terrible silence, and then:

A blue 101 warhead!

SOUHAYLA: Ahaaaa! For fuck's sake! This has to end!

SOUHAYLA gets to her feet. NEYIF enters and puts down some bags, then exits quickly.

Why are you attacking us! There must be some mistake! A terrible misunderstanding, diplomacy gone wrong – talk to your superiors, this is all just a big joke.

A violent explosion.

NEYIF: (*Entering and putting down some more bags.*) I'll go and get the sleeping bags. Everyone get ready to leave.

Two violent explosions force him to lie down.

NEEL: Papa!

NAZHA: Nelly!

SOUHAYLA: Stop! (*A violent explosion.*) Listen to me! (*A violent explosion.*) My name is Souhayla… (*A violent explosion.*) And I want to get married! (*Two violent explosions.*) Does anyone want to be my husband? (*A violent explosion.*) I'm 34 but I have nice soft skin! My teeth are bad but I have a very sweet personality (*Three violent explosions.*) I do housework, I do dishes, I can sew (*A violent explosion.*) I have a sense of humour, I'm cultured (*Two violent explosions.*) I have everything it takes to make a man happy (*A violent explosion.*) – a beautiful smile, a nice mouth, large tits (*A violent explosion.*) a big arse (*A violent explosion.*) and I'm still a virgin!(*A violent explosion.*) Is there really no one on this whole fucking godforsaken planet who wants to marry me?!

A violent explosion.

NEYIF: Everything's ready. Let's go.

NAZHA: We've got to do something. They're gonna get themselves killed.

NEYIF: Souhayla! Nelly! Hurry! We've got to go downstairs! (*A violent explosion forces NEYIF to lie down.*). Nelly! The bombs!

SOUHAYLA: Nelly, your fiancé won't come, he's probably changed his mind.

NELLY: My fiancé will come.

A violent explosion.

SOUHAYLA: It's raining bombs! How can he come?

A violent explosion.

NELLY: The bombs are nothing. A bit of wind. The bombs don't know anything, but I know a poem by my brother.

A violent explosion.

SOUHAYLA: A poem?

NEYIF: I'm going to count to three, then we'll grab them and force them out with us.

Distant explosions.

NELLY: A poem.

NEYIF: Let's go!

NEYIF, NAZHA and NEEL come out of their hiding places and grab NELLY, lift her off the ground. As they lift her, a bomb explodes right outside the window and lights up the whole apartment.

NELLY: Today I walk,
I walk, and in my head
And in my heart
I remember!
A love is born.
At the detour of a road
I kissed her lips.

The day has risen.
In my hands, your marvellous face!
Three birds take flight!
I smile,
I smile,
I smile with joy.

NELLY falls into NEEL's arms. Silence. No more bombs. Nothing.
A knock on the door.

SOUHAYLA: The guests!

NAZHA: My God! The guests!

There is another knock.

NEYIF: It's so quiet.

SOUHAYLA: People must be crazy to leave home when it's like this outside!

NEYIF: It's so quiet.

NEEL: You're so pale, Nelly!

NELLY: My heart is beating so fast!

NEYIF: I'm not hungry anymore. I'm not hungry anymore.

Another knock. NAZHA opens the door. A man enters. He is smiling.
He is well-dressed.

Neatly. He is a foreigner. He is handsome.

NAZHA: Sir?

GENTLEMAN: Bonjour, Madame.

Gentleman offers a bouquet of daisies to NAZHA.

SOUHAYLA: The fiancé!

GENTLEMAN: You must be the charming neighbour. Souhayla, isn't it?

SOUHAYLA: The fiancé! It's the fiancé! At last! ... Yes... hurray...hurray... It's the fiancé!

NEYIF: Well!

NEEL: Who is this guy?

GENTLEMAN: Hello, Neel!

NEEL: Who is this guy?

SOUHAYLA: Ah! You know…don't worry, they're a little bit, in shock, you know…how can I explain… But they've been waiting for you since this morning…you didn't have too much trouble finding the house?

GENTLEMAN: A couple of fishermen showed me the way.

NAZHA: I don't feel very well…

NEYIF: This is incredible!

SOUHAYLA: But what's the matter with you? The fiancé is here, the party can get started!

NEEL: Fucking hell! It's François.

NEYIF: This is insane!

SOUHAYLA: You managed to avoid the areas that were too heavily bombed? Good for you! Oh, you!! With this storm on top of everything you must be soaked!

GENTLEMAN: The storm? What storm? There was a clear blue sky! The storm!… I didn't hear a thing! Bombing, you say? Why would there be bombing? There was a very slight breeze! You have a delightful country. These trees, this sea, oh, this sea!!

NEEL: Holy shit!

NAZHA: Do you know us?

GENTLEMAN: I recognize you.

NEEL: Papa, Papa, it's François!

NAZHA: Why have you come?

NEYIF: Oh my God, I'm not hungry anymore!

NEEL: It's François!

SOUHAYLA: I don't understand anything anymore. Is this gentleman a guest, or is he the fiancé?

NAZHA: There isn't any fiancé! There never was a fiancé, We made the whole thing up to pass the time, to relieve our boredom a little. There can never be a fiancé.

GENTLEMAN: Oh, yes, I am the fiancé – if Nelly will have me.

NELLY: Yes, I'll have you, sir.

NEEL: Fucking hell…it's François. It's really François!

NELLY: Mama! The guests will be here soon! You'll say goodbye to them for us! I'm leaving! Celebrate!

NAZHA: Nelly!

NELLY: I'm awake, Mama! You should be happy! Tomorrow you'll walk with your head held high! You'll have married off your daughter! Rejoice! I've awakened!

GENTLEMAN: Goodbye, Madame, Monsieur. See you soon, Neel. Goodbye, Souhayla!

SOUHAYLA: Oh! You!

NEYIF: Take care, Nelly! Be happy!

NAZHA: Be happy? Yes, be happy, Nelly!

NELLY: Farewell, Mama, farewell, Papa.

NEEL: You're so lucky Nelly! You're going to live in a country where the main concern is the fight against pornography in primary schools! The people there are so happy!

NELLY: Don't forget, Neel! My little brother, my consolation, my joy, I predict, yes I predict that your bones will grow and burst open your coffin, your bones will slowly grow upwards, turning into an ancient cedar! Later on people will come and make love in the shade of your branches!

GENTLEMAN: Let us go!

NAZHA: Where are you going?

GENTLEMAN: To a villa by the sea. But beforehand we'll drive over to Berdawnay to eat kneffay. It's Friday.

NELLY and the fiancé exit.

NEEL: I'm going to close the window!

More gunshots. One very precise one. The window shatters. NEEL reels and falls on the wedding table. Silence. Nobody moves.

NAZHA: Neel!

NEYIF: Neel! Neel!

NEEL: M.16, new version!

NAZHA: It'll be alright! Don't move! It's nothing! It's nothing!

NEEL: I told you it was going to start the same way!

NAZHA: Get up, my baby! Get up! Come, we'll get those potatoes fried, come, my darling! Oh no, no, no, no, I don't want you to… Get up, get up, get up!

NEEL: You know what I'd like?

NAZHA: My little prince!

NEEL: To play 'Tickle my…'

NEYIF: I don't know how to play.

NEEL: Souhayla knows.

SOUHAYLA: Once upon a time there was…

NEEL: Tickle my fuzz…

SOUHAYLA: A boy full of fun…

NEEL: Tickle my bun…

SOUHAYLA: He was cute as could be…

NEEL: Tickle my knee…

SOUHAYLA: And he loved a good trick…

NEEL: Tickle my dick…

SOUHAYLA: Till one day in the rain…

NEEL: Tickle my brain…

SOUHAYLA: A bee-sting made him quiver…

NEEL: Tickle my liver…

SOUHAYLA: And by his father's side…

NEEL: Tickle my hide…

A bomb explodes with distinction.

A shining coral, quick, a wish…

SOUHAYLA: He breathed his last.

NEEL: Tickle my ARSE!

NEEL dies.

The End

Glossary

Ya aybeyshoom: Means something akin to 'what a disgrace!';
Pronounciation: rhymes with 'but why fey broom' (ya ay' bey
shoom).

Arak: An anise-flavoured liqueur. Rhymes with 'a rack' (a rak'.).

Baba ghanouj: A pureed aubergine dip for pita bread.

Battenjen: Aubergine. Rhymes with 'buttonmen' (bat' tenjen.).

Beyleywa: Baklava; a desert made from filopastry, honey and nuts.
The first two syllables rhyme with 'hey', the last rhymes with
'pah'. There is also a glottal stop after the first syllable (Bey' ley
wa).

Berdawnay: A beautiful small resort town in Lebanon. Rhymes
with 'Bear down, May' (Ber daw' nay).

Coussa: Courgette. (Pron: Koo' suh).

Fassoulia: a white bean dish with a tomato-garlic sauce. (Pron. Fuh
soo' lya.).

Hummus: A dip for pita made from pureed chick peas, tahini,
garlic and lemon.

Keshk: Tiny dumplings stuffed with ground beef in a spiced yogurt
sauce (Pron: Kesh' k.).

Kneffay: A traditional Lebanese dessert of stuffed shredded whaet
in a rosewater and lemon syrup.(Pron: kne' ffay.).

Mamelukes: Military class that ruled Egypt from 1254 to 1811
(Pron: Ma' me lukes.).

Mssayadiyay: A traditional Lebanese fish dish. (Pron: Sigh aw' dee
yay.).

Tabbouleh: A Lebanese salad of parsley and bulgar wheat with a
lemon dressing. (Pron. Ta boo' leh.).

Warra Arreesh: Traditional Lebanese dish of vine leaves stuffed
with beef and rice. (Pron. wa rra a rreesh.) There is a half-stress
after the first syllable, and the double r's are trilled.